EVERYDAY CULTURE

EVERYDAY CULTURE

FINDING AND MAKING MEANING IN A CHANGING WORLD

DAVID TREND

Paradigm Publishers
Boulder • London

Paradigm Publishers is committed to preserving ancient forests and natural resources. We elected to print *Everyday Culture* on 50% post consumer recycled paper, processed chlorine free. As a result, for this printing, we have saved:

6 Trees (40' tall and 6-8" diameter)
2,358 Gallons of Wastewater
948 Kilowatt Hours of Electricity
260 Pounds of Solid Waste
511 Pounds of Greenhouse Gases

Paradigm Publishers made this paper choice because our printer, Thomson-Shore, Inc., is a member of Green Press Initiative, a nonprofit program dedicated to supporting authors, publishers, and suppliers in their efforts to reduce their use of fiber obtained from endangered forests.

For more information, visit www.greenpressinitiative.org

Copyright © 2007 Paradigm Publishers

Published in the United States by Paradigm Publishers, 3360 Mitchell Lane Suite E, Boulder, CO 80301 USA.

Paradigm Publishers is the trade name of Birkenkamp & Company, LLC, Dean Birkenkamp, President and Publisher.

Library of Congress Cataloging-in-Publication Data
Trend, David.
Everyday culture : finding and making meaning in a changing world / David Trend.
        p. cm.
Includes bibliographical references and index.
ISBN 978-1-59451-426-5 (hardcover : alk. paper)
ISBN 978-1-59451-427-2 (pbk. : alk. paper)
    1. Social change. 2. Culture. I. Title.
HM831.T75 2007
306.4068—dc22

                                              200701967

Printed and bound in the United States of America on acid free paper that meets the standards of the American National Standard for Permanence of Paper for Printed Library Materials.

Designed and Typeset by Straight Creek Bookmakers

11 10 09 08 07 1 2 3 4 5

Contents

PREFACE: EVERYDAY CULTURE

Everyday Culture draws its inspiration from a particular historical moment. In 1968, the meanings and potentials of ordinary life received attention in cultural and political circles throughout the western world as never before. Radios were playing "Everyday People," a song by the rock/funk band Sly & the Family Stone. Released in the months following the infamous Tet Offensive in Vietnam and the assassination of Dr. Martin Luther King, Jr., "Everyday People" captured the spirit of American culture as a plea for peace and equality. Remembered for its chorus, "I am everyday people," the song resonates in a celebration of diversity, as lead singer Sly Stone Stewart proclaims, "We are the same whatever we do," with the refrain, "We've got to live together." "Everyday People" holds the distinction as the first hit song in the United States by a multiracial performing group.

As "Everyday People" was rising on U.S. pop charts, a more material manifestation of the everyday was taking hold in Europe. In May 1968, a general strike erupted in France within universities and high schools in a series of uprisings, protesting poor wages and governmental wrongdoing. The riots outside the Sorbonne, in Paris, included workers, minorities, the French Communist party, and members of Situationist Internationale. Within a week, France was crippled by a work stoppage that involved ten million people—roughly two-thirds of the nation's labor force—making it the largest strike in recorded history.

Inspired in part by these historical legacies, *Everyday Culture* is about the confluence of cultural and material possibility—the bringing together of thought and action in daily life. This book argues that an informed and invigorated citizenry can help reverse patterns of dehumanization and social injustice. The impetus for *Everyday Culture* can be described in the observation by the British post-war theorist Raymond Williams that "culture is ordinary," and that the fabric of meanings that inform and organize everyday life often go undervalued and unexamined.[1] *Everyday Culture* shares with thinkers such as Williams the conviction that it is precisely the ordinariness of culture that makes it extraordinarily important. The ubiquity of everyday culture means that it affects all aspects of contemporary economic, social, and political life. Seen in this light, *Everyday Culture* is about a hope for a better future.

David Trend

Note

1. Raymond Williams, "Culture is Ordinary," *Resources of Hope: Reflections on Culture, Socialism, and Democracy* (London: Verso, 1958).

Chapter One
Beginning

An Introduction

We begin with what we know. In the classic study, *The Practice of Everyday Life,* which was published in English in 1984, Michel de Certeau draws a distinction between the acquisition and the use of knowledge. A great believer in the intellectual capacities of ordinary people, de Certeau recognized that individuals had skills for critical thinking and understanding the world around them. Yet de Certeau wondered why groups living in poor conditions or under the authority of unreasonable leaders would continue to do so without complaint. The answer, he speculated, had something to do with a disconnection between knowledge of these poor conditions and the act of doing something to change them. De Certeau and many political theorists of his generation concluded that people could benefit from education about the practical skills and strategies needed to change their lives. To that end, de Certeau wrote that "we must determine the procedures, bases, effects, and possibilities of this collective activity."[1]

Everyday Culture: Finding Meaning in a Changing World is about this ongoing quest for solutions to social problems and strategies for positive social change. The book addresses key themes in the study of contemporary communications: the relationships among media, art, and culture; concepts of audience; differing functions of mass communication forms; new information technologies; education and democracy; and issues of identity, difference, and globalization. Often the general public thinks that mass media are all-powerful and that "art" exists only in museums and has little to do with their personal interests. This book challenges these assumptions by examining media and art in the broader contexts of culture and everyday life. Addressing the many institutions and interests that shape what people listen to, watch on TV, or play on their computers, *Everyday Culture* puts culture in familiar terms by talking about life at work, at school, and at home. In doing this, discussions in the book center around the role of media culture in our understandings of who we are, how we got here, the kind of world we'd like to inhabit, and how we might get to that place.

Everyday Culture asserts that we live in a time in which the everyday cultural activities that fill our lives are largely undervalued and ignored. The things that occupy our time, give us enjoyment, and dominate much of our thinking—reading books, pursuing hobbies, listening to music, watching television, sending e-mail, talking with friends, or sharing meals—are considered by most of us to have little to do with the larger economic circumstances that influence our standard of living, the political forces that determine our rights and our codes of behavior, or the global interests that influence foreign policy, war, and peace. But these things that occupy most of our time and thoughts may also include the daily rituals of school, work, religious observances, commuting, shopping, running errands, and executing household chores.

Everyday Culture takes a critical look at why most people feel powerless and cut off from the "bigger" forces that govern our lives. At no other time in recent decades have people felt more disconnected from government, large institutions, and the media conglomerates. Multinational manufacturers and retail chains limit choice and diversity in what we eat, wear, and consume. Educational authorities and media experts deplore the activities and entertainment that most people enjoy. Bureaucrats and government officials waste tax revenues, enact frivolous legislation, and declare unwanted wars. In the face of powerlessness and detachment from public life, large segments of the population have become alienated from politics, disillusioned with the democratic process, and absorbed with self-interest and private concerns.

History and the "Everyday"

These perceptions of omniscient authority aren't especially new. Many of them originated with the social reorganization of the modern enlightenment beginning in the 1500s. The era and its ethos of human "progress" celebrated objectivity, reason, and rigidly structured living over the subjectivity, intuitiveness, and organic societies that preceded it in the Middle Ages. The new era brought with it the categorization of ideas into disciplines of intellectual specialization such as science, history, and mathematics, as well as distinctions between high and low culture. The enlightenment also coincided with the development of trade and capitalism, which brought with them the commodification of goods and human labor. The transformation of craft labor into factory work under capitalism meant that things like shoes and crops were no longer simply produced for their use or enjoyment but for their exchange value for other goods. Work drained of its creative spirit became something one sold. With the rise of industry in the late modern era, control became more mechanized. The repetition inherent to industrial production made work boring. Describing work on the assembly line, Karl Marx wrote in 1867, "Here is the movement of the machine he must follow."[2] The ethos of control—what Max Weber called the "iron cage" of bureaucratic rationality—extended outside the workplace and into all aspects of life.[3]

As more and more parts of life fell subject to bureaucratic organization, time became something people measured and worried about. New technologies of time played a role in this process, such as the development of clocks in the fourteenth century. The growing mechanization of time measurement resulted in an abstraction of its duration—no longer tying it to external events like waking or sunrise. The ability to measure time allowed people to become more conscious of it, calling attention to how much time was spent at work, school, church, or in leisure activities. Time also became geographically synchronized as never before. Prior to the nineteenth century, people reset their pocket watches when traveling according to local time standards, which varied from place to place. The growth of railroad travel and the near-instantaneous communication of the telegraph allowed the synchronization of time between towns and cites.

The standardization of time and its growing presence in people's lives contributed to new means of control and the standardization of identity itself. Eventually, the objectification of work and leisure began to influence the way people perceived themselves. Rather than identifying themselves as autonomous subjects who acted upon the world and made it their own, people saw themselves as passive objects. Work became time that one "owed" to someone else, or work was a way a person "marked" time. Time off the job and not well "spent" became "wasted time." As a highly structured and manipulated experience, leisure time became a site of pseudo-enjoyment, or what one writer termed "organized passivity."[4]

The pessimism of this perspective was codified in the 1930s and 1940s by the Marxist thinkers of the Frankfurt School, who wrote of the manipulation of the "masses." Writers Max Horkheimer and Theodor Adorno asserted that people were powerless to resist the overwhelming forces of capitalism, its seductive ideology of consumption, and the continuous desire for more material goods.[5] Within this logic, people became ensnared by an endless cycle of working and spending. To the Frankfurt School, the mass media played a central role in convincing people to accept the "false consciousness" that made them passively accept their oppressive lives.

This negative view does not end the story. Other groups of intellectuals argued that the grasp of ideology could never be so absolute and that people always retained critical capacities to question and contest false consciousness. To the Situationists, this liberating consciousness lay embedded within everyday experience that no authority could ever completely control. Intellectuals Henri Lefebvre and Guy Debord argued that the very quality of the "everyday" could rescue people from mass oppression due to the individualistic ways that people experience life.[6] People are too different and complex to be manipulated uniformly by monolithic institutions and discourses. Summarizing the sentiments of these writers, Michael E. Gardiner wrote that although it remains possible that the "complexity, the depth of experience, and intensity of interpersonal relationships located within everyday life will be impoverished, this sphere also contains resistant or counterhegemonic qualities that point toward the possibility of radical disalienation and full humanization of social life."[7]

But how do we work toward a society that is more geared toward connectivity and engagement? Throughout the twentieth century, artists have sought to recapture everyday experience by drawing attention to its overlooked aspects or by portraying the everyday in unusual ways. Avant-gardists in Europe and the United States used various techniques to identify details, objects, or experiences from daily life that could convey extraordinary or transcendental value, or that simply would remind viewers of the intrinsic aesthetics of common experience. Some artists made artworks from "found objects" ranging from household utensils to industrial machines in assemblage sculptures. Surrealists of the early 1900s used bits of text and imagery from newspapers and magazines in collages. Members of the French Lettrist movement took these impulses even further in their fragmentation of words, recontextuallization of alphabetic symbols, and experiments with typography and numerology. Radical performers enacted plays, "happenings," or other events in the streets to break down conventional understandings of what art was and where it was seen.

Many of these ideas were brought together in the writings of Michel de Certeau, who believed strongly in the liberating potential inherent in everyday activities. Unlike many of his generation who argued that consumer culture held a tyrannizing grip on the public, de Certeau encouraged people to appropriate and reuse materials around them for their own purposes. Rather than giving in to the mandates and rules of bureaucratic authority and mind-numbing conformity, de Certeau urged people to find ways to subvert the given order—a resistant impulse he believed was inherent in everyday existence. Commercial culture was not something to be feared. Besides, de Certeau argued, it was beyond escape. Instead, de Certeau recommended finding "ways of using the products imposed by the dominant economic order."[8] "Creativity is the act of reusing and recombining heterogeneous materials," he wrote.[9]

In contrast to many of his leftist contemporaries, de Certeau argued that resistance was not limited to direct action and economic struggle. Politics also resided in cultural works and forms of expression. Although de Certeau never abandoned material causes, he argued that the separation of the text from materiality was a false distinction. Production and consumption should not be seen as separate realms any more than reading and writing. He wrote, "We have to quit thinking that a qualitative gap exists between the acts of reading and writing. The first is a silent creativity invested in what the reader does with the text; the second is the very creativity, but made more explicit in the production of a new text."[10]

As de Certeau's thinking on appropriation and language might suggest, he saw great potential for resistance in modest everyday moments. To him, power was not only exerted upon people in many aspects of their lives—it also could be resisted in even the smallest activity. This was the basis for de Certeau's famous distinction between a "strategy" enacted as a general rule, typically from an authoritarian body, and a "tactic" issued as localized struggle from a subordinated entity. The importance of de Certeau's work for *Everyday Culture* lies in the encouragement it gives in a world where people often feel alienated and removed from the forces that govern their lives. Government, the legislature, huge corporations, and educational institutions may seem beyond the reach of individuals. But to de Certeau, revolution can begin in small places. The desire for change is what is most important. The program for that change begins with something as simple as a conversation with a friend or an action taken by a small group.

Everyday Culture: Finding Meaning in a Changing World begins with a discussion about everyday life, providing readers a fuller understanding of how underexamined aspects of daily existence can provide insights into larger issues that affect who we are, the groups to which we belong, the social circumstances in which we find ourselves, and the economic and political circumstances that determine what we can do and who we can become. Then, the book explores more specific aspects of empowerment within these groups, situations, and organizations.

One key strategy of exploring empowerment is to engage, more critically, all those things that work against people's ability to see themselves as subjects. For this reason, *Everyday Culture* spends a great deal of time looking at ways of interpreting media and "reading" the world of advertising, entertainment, news, and consumerism that so influences how we think and feel. Next comes a consideration of the moral and political implications of this inquiry. This means asking how ideas and actions affect other people and how those ideas and actions form structures and policies that perpetuate their effects. Such a spirit of ethical concern stems from the recognition of the connectedness between all people and the realization that an injury to one person is an injury to all humanity. This is an important counterpoint to the critical individualism that a focus on the everyday can sometimes imply. But this ethical approach to living should not be confused with a unifying moral or religious program. It is a morality that reflects the diverse and complex histories of all peoples. Its only unifying principle is the concern for others and the respect it generates for difference and egalitarianism.

How the Book Is Organized

Everyday Culture is designed to function primarily as a practical guide and resource for an enlivened and critically informed experience of the everyday. The book offers a variety of approaches to different aspects of the everyday experience. *Everyday Culture* includes discussions of prominent thinkers about everyday life, considerations of activities that make up daily life, and examinations of topics in popular culture, media, and consumption. *Everyday Culture* is divided into five chapters, each of which addresses major themes: "Asking," "Reading," "Finding," "Joining," and "Building."

Each chapter contains several essays on topics relevant to that particular theme but not intended to exhaust it. For example, Chapter 2, "Asking: Questioning Culture and Consumption," contains an essay entitled "Everyday Culture," which examines different definitions and types of culture. Another essay, "But Is It Art?" looks at fine art as a special case of culture. The article "What Everybody Wants" outlines a range of approaches to the understanding of consumer culture.

Theoretical principles are woven throughout the book in an effort to attach ideas to their practical applications—an approach in keeping with the immediacy and hands-on character of everyday experience. The thinkers discussed in *Everyday Culture* include such diverse personalities as Judith Butler, Michel Foucault, Henry Giroux, Stuart Hall, bell hooks, Lucy Lippard, Henri Lefebvre, Kobena Mercer, Trinh T. Minh-Ha, Juliet Schor, Raymond Williams, and Paul Willis. As these names suggest, this volume takes a necessarily interdisciplinary approach to everyday culture—a topic that resists easy or conventional categorizations—addressing it from the perspectives of communications, cultural studies, critical pedagogy, multiculturalism, and women's studies, among other areas of inquiry.

Chapter 2 examines the mental processes (ideas, languages, historical understandings, ideologies, habits of mind, belief systems) and material circumstances (tools, belongings, physical structures, institutions, governments) that identify and locate us in our world. We will approach culture broadly as the sum total of these structuring and meaning-producing processes. Chapter 3, "Reading: Language, Communication, and New Media," addresses various forms that culture takes: as idea and object, as rarified practice and everyday activity, as a vehicle of creative self-expression, and as a tool of manipulation. The forms of culture are played out differently in different cultural activities—shopping, going to school, traveling, working, and enjoying leisure time—as well as different media—movies, books, TV shows, video games, magazines, and the Internet. Building on these topics, Chapter 4, "Finding: Self and Identity," looks at processes of self-discovery and the individual, and asks: Who do you think you are? What are the circumstances and forces that shape self-concept? What forms of learning inform our understandings of ourselves? Next, Chapter 5, "Joining: Communities and Publics," discusses groups, collective understandings, institutions, and life in the public realm. It examines the roles that audiences play in making things famous, in responding to marketing campaigns, or in taking part in elections. The book concludes with the chapter "Building: Globalization and Democracy," which discusses our roles as citizens of nations and the world. By reaffirming the old dictum "think globally, act locally," we can focus on the way our everyday actions at home, school, with friends, or at a job affect democracy on local levels, and we can look at how those actions can help us begin thinking about equality and social change in the larger world.

In summary, the simple premise of *Everyday Culture* is that our perceived disconnection from larger cultural, economic, and political spheres is a fiction. People actually have a great deal to say about large institutional and intellectual spheres—but they have become convinced that they don't. Consumer boycotts can change the way large corporations act and the kind of items stores such as Wal-Mart and Costco sell. Letter-writing campaigns and voter activism really can alter the behavior of a legislator or put a member of congress out of office. Massive citizen action can alter tax policy and influence the way our government treats other nations. And these bigger changes don't need to begin with huge numbers of people. They can start with something as simple as a discussion over the dinner table tonight or a meeting one decides to have with a teacher or group of friends. This book is about the relationship between these everyday activities, our attitudes toward them, and our understanding of the way they relate to that larger world.

Notes

1. Michel de Certeau, *The Practice of Everyday Life,* trans. Steven Randall (Berkeley and Los Angeles: University of California Press, 1984), xiv.

2. Karl Marx, *Capital Vol. 1,* trans. Ben Fowkes (New York: Penguin, 1967), 548.

3. Max Weber, *The Protestant Ethic and the Spirit of Capitalism (1904–1905)* (New York: Routledge, 2001), 24.

4. Michael E. Gardiner, *Critiques of Everyday Life* (London and New York: Routledge, 2000), 14.

5. Max Horkheimer and Theodore Adorno, *The Dialectic of Enlightment,* trans. John Cumming (New York: Herder and Herder, 1972).

6. Henri Lefebvre, *Dialectical Materialism,* trans. J. Sturrock (London and New York: Jonathan Cape, 1988); Guy Debord, *The Society of the Spectacle and Other Films,* trans. K. Sandborn and R. Parry (London: Rebel Press, 1992).

7. Gardiner, 17.

8. de Certeau, *The Practice of Everyday Life,* xiii.

9. Michel de Certeau, *Culture in the Plural,* trans. Tom Conley (Minneapolis: University of Minnesota, 1997), 49.

10. de Certeau, *Culture in the Plural,* 145.

Chapter Two
Asking

Questioning Culture and Consumption

Asking is no simple matter. The answers we get are determined by the questions we ask. So asking questions is not an innocent process. What are the mental processes (ideas, languages, historical understandings, ideologies, habits of mind, belief systems) and material circumstances (tools, belongings, physical structures, institutions, governments) that identify and locate us in our world? Asking such questions in this section, we will approach culture broadly, as the various structuring and meaning-producing circumstances imply.

Some of the answers to these questions come from the perspective of "cultural studies," an approach to knowledge that interrogates the practices, schools of thought, and institutions that give ideas legitimacy. A relatively new field of study, cultural studies is one of the few areas within colleges and universities that takes everyday culture seriously.

As described by Raymond Williams, one of cultural studies' early theorists, the discipline looks at the broad array of "works" (artworks, material culture, media, popular entertainment) and "group behaviors"(school, work, leisure activities, religious observances).[1] Within Williams's definition of cultural studies, culture is not something "out there" in a museum. It's something that we know and experience all the time. Cultural studies also critiques concepts of "high" and "low" culture, and these are defined in the following section, "Everyday Culture." Such distinctions often serve to divide culture along lines of education, social class, age, and ethnicity.

Much of the discussion in this section will address ongoing debates over everyday culture between proponents of elitism and egalitarianism. While this might seem like a debate long settled in modern democratic societies, the issue of elitism and its presumed benefit continues to fester in the background of everyday culture—often in coded discussions about education, affirmative action, immigration, and tax legislation, which allow deep-seated prejudices and beliefs to be masked in bureaucratic debate. Lacking even a hint of irony, this platform for elitism was assembled in a book by former *Time* magazine cultural critic William Henry III. Entitled *In Defense of Elitism,* the volume begins with the assertion that in all the major public policy debates of the last half-century between elites and egalitarians, the latter have been winning far too often.[2] This arises from a few beliefs that Henry asserts have become widespread: that all people are basically the same; that the common man is unerring and needs no intermediaries; that self-expression and self-esteem are more important than objective achievement; and that a good and just society ought to spend more of its time and energy propping up the "losers" than in encouraging the "winners." To Henry and his fellow reactionaries, the modest advances made in recent decades by equal rights and affirmative action have so threatened the centuries-old bastions of wealth and privilege that they demand immediate assault. Henry's rants might be dismissed immediately if they weren't so popular. Unfortunately, such reactionary thinking is amplified through the likes of Sean Hannity, Rush Limbaugh, Lou Dobbs, and other media personalities.

"Asking: Questioning Culture and Consumption" opens with an essay entitled "Everyday Culture," which provides background for the sections to follow and examines different definitions and types of culture. The section also includes an introductory discussion of cultural studies. The next essay, "But Is it Art?" looks at fine art as a special case of culture with its own history and set of analytical problems. Conventional stereotypes about art are contrasted with a variety of common and uncommon uses to which fine art has been applied. The section concludes with the article "What Everybody Wants," outlining a range of approaches to the understanding of consumer culture.

Everyday Culture

The term "high culture" often refers to forms of culture that a society categorizes as significant: valuable works of art, great books, specialized aesthetic knowledge. By its very definition, the production of high culture is deemed beyond the creative capabilities of ordinary people. It is made by specialists or experts—and appreciated by people with education or elevated status. As such, what constitutes high culture generally gets determined by those who hold authority in a society. As sociologist Howard Becker explains,

> High culture consists of work recognized as belonging to an honored category of cultural understandings by people who have the power to make that determination and to have it accepted by others. We may be able to devise systematic criteria that will identify work of superior quality, but it is unlikely that the work we can distinguish in that way will be the same as work

legitimated as high culture by the institutions that make that decision for any society.[3]

The idiosyncratic system that identifies and validates high culture is hardly harmless or innocent. It supports dominant ethnic and racial groups in a nation and excludes the culture brought by immigrants or newcomers. Within this system, everyday culture often is regarded as something "left over." Anthropologist Pierre Bourdieu wrote that high culture is frequently regarded as something that engages the mind and serves nonutilitarian interest.[4] As Bourdieu wrote in *Distinction,* his study of the way class shapes cultural preferences or taste, "There is nothing automatic or natural about the ability to 'appreciate' a Rembrandt or a Picasso. You must be raised to feel comfortable in museums" and have what Bourdieu saw as the "educated bourgeois orientation" associated with leisure, money, and unselfconscious social privilege.[5] By contrast, Bourdieu wrote that "low" or popular culture appeals to the unschooled interests of the body. Regardless of background or schooling, anyone can enjoy raucous humor, rock and roll, or a slice of pizza.

Some proponents of high culture assert that its values should be universally adopted in the interest of social cohesion. In representing the "best" instances of thought and artistic expression, works of high culture set examples for everyone to recognize and emulate. The more a society embraces a common set of high cultural values and standards, the more unified and strong it becomes.[6] Societies that allow people to consume a hodge-podge of different cultural influences and subscribe to varied standards of what is "good" and "bad" culture risk falling into chaos and instability. This argument can be summarized in terms of what some writers have termed "cultural relativism"—the belief that cultural differences (like those that come from varied nationalities and ethnicities) are not neutral in value.[7] Differences dilute the virtue and coherence that hold a society together, resulting in what some have termed a "Babel" effect of cultural incoherence.[8]

Of course, in a nation such as the United States, which itself is made up of people from many different places and backgrounds, the stratification of culture into high and low registers is a tricky logical maneuver. Like most dichotomies that attempt to divide the world into either/or categories, the high/low divide is at best an abstraction. In practice, neither category is neat or distinct; many items fall into either or both sides—or simply resist classification altogether. In this way, the high/low divide is a cultural construction that really represents other hierarchies, imbalances, and prejudices. The United States is itself a hybrid of cultures. Proponents of high culture in this country often see themselves on a quest for a purely "American" culture defined by standards set by the majority. This desire for cultural conformity was exactly the sort of thinking that troubled Alexis de Tocqueville when he wrote his 1835 critique of U.S. politics, *Democracy in America*. While acknowledging that one social power may inevitably dominate others, de Tocqueville was concerned about an apparatus that permitted what he termed "the tyranny of the majority." Such a system generates "a power which is physical and moral at the same time; it acts upon the will as well as upon the actions of men, and it represents not only all contest, but all controversy. I know of no country in which there is so little true independence of mind and freedom of discussion as in America."[9]

The result, de Tocqueville noted, is a privileging of English-speaking culture over all others. Beyond its obvious deleterious effects on excluded groups, the trouble with this narrow view is that even its proponents cannot agree about the best of what has been thought or said. Even the staid pages of the *New York Times* reported that "the idea of a literature as a fixed and immutable canon—the Great Books, five-foot shelf—is a historical illusion."[10]

In the 1990s, academics of all disciplines and ideologies began challenging the primacy of the Euro-American standard, just as they now are disputing traditional definitions of what constitutes literature in the first place. As the late Roland Barthes wrote, the challenge begins in pointing out what falls outside traditional formulations. "Education should be directed toward exploring the literary text as much as possible. The pedagogical problem would be to shake up the notion of the literary text and to make adolescents understand that there is text everywhere," Barthes said.[11]

Received Culture and Identity

Most cultural understandings come to us from learned experiences. The sources of these experiences are diverse, including those occurring at home, in school, with friends, or at the workplace. To a large extent, we gain our identities from these "real" experiences and from simulations of experiences received from books, magazines, television, movies, and the Internet. Male and female identity, for example, originate in the context of family life and social interaction—later to be reinforced in images. Much has been written about the way gender is portrayed in the media. In *Ways of Seeing,* a book based on a BBC television series, John Berger wrote that "according to usage and conventions which are at last being questioned but have by no means been overcome—*men act* and *women appear.* Men look at women. Women watch themselves being looked at."[12] Berger asserted that in European art beginning with the seventh century, women were depicted as being aware of being seen by a male spectator. Paintings of female nudes reflected the woman's submission to "the owner of both woman and painting."[13] He noted that almost all European sexual imagery since the Renaissance is frontal—either literally or metaphorically—because the viewer is the spectator-owner doing the looking.

During the 1970s and 1980s, feminist media critics similarly observed that much photography, television, and film reflects a male point of view. This gendered perspective is not only a factor of historical habit, but also a reflection of the predominance of men in the media industries. Some observers have gone as far as to say that when women look at clothing and cosmetic ads, they are actually seeing themselves as a man might see a woman. Laura Mulvey, writing in her classic essay "Visual Pleasure and Narrative Cinema," asserted that traditional films present men as active, controlling subjects and treat women as passive objects of desire for men in both the story and in the audience, and do not allow women to be desiring subjects in their own right.[14] Such films objectify women in relation to "the controlling male gaze, presenting woman as image and man as bearer of the look."[15]

National identity is another form of received culture. One is reminded of being a resident in the United States by the federal institutions that deliver our mail, collect taxes, enforce the nation's borders, and provide military protection. As with gender, perceptions of national identity also come from the media. In his book *Imagined Communities: Reflections on the Origin and Spread of Nationalism,* Benedict Anderson argued that the invention of the printing press first permitted national borders to be drawn that were not defined by geographical boundaries like oceans or mountain ranges.[16] As Anderson put it, "an American will never meet, or even know the names of more than a handful of his fellow Americans. He has no idea of what they are up to at any one time. But he has complete confidence in their steady, anonymous, simultaneous activity."[17] The circulation of printed material within countries enabled citizens to be continually reminded of their identities as citizens. Homi K. Bhabha has gone as far as to say that the continuing renewal of national identity—the will to nationhood that is reaffirmed each day—requires an erasure of past origins, ethnicities, and places. The obligation to forget in the name of unity is a form of "violence involved in establishing the national writ."[18] Movies and television deliver this message. The power of media to influence national identity became a topic of international interest in the twentieth century as the United States emerged as an exporter of television and film around the globe. The ability to broadcast across national boundaries, even in the face of government resistance, motivated the electronic warfare waged by the U.S. Information Agency in nations around the world.

Of course, media imperialism isn't always so belligerent. On the contrary, the mass marketing of U.S. productions throughout the world is customarily viewed as a positive function of the "free market." Due to the scale and technical sophistication of the American media industry, Hollywood films and television programs constitute the nation's second-largest source of foreign income, just behind aerospace technology.[19] Moreover, the mass dissemination of U.S. movies and TV abroad helped provide an important context for the foreign consumption of American products—from McDonald's in Russia to Marlboros in Thailand to Euro-Disney in France. Although this ability to profit in the media trade helps the nation's sagging economy, the massive influx of American media into other nations is not always viewed as a positive phenomenon. Familiar figures such as Britney Spears, glowing on television screens throughout Europe, Africa, and Asia, have triggered mass resentment about the transmission of Yankee culture throughout the globe. Consequently, government-sponsored media education programs in nations that import significant amounts of film and television are far more advanced than in the United States. Foreign nations perceive the need to protect themselves from the boundless expansion of American capitalism. As a result, Canada, China, and France, to name a few countries, put national quotas on the amount of American media that can be broadcast to their people. In recent decades, the so-called imperialism of American media has become less absolute. With the growth and diffusion of film and television from other industrialized nations, media culture has begun to move in a more reciprocal manner. This phenomenon has been helped along by patterns of migration that have created more diverse audiences around the world. Technology has played a role as well in the expansion of videotape, disc, and Internet media formats.

Almost since the inception of television, a diverse assortment of educators, parents, and religious groups has warned of the corrupting influence of commercial media. Like critics of media dissemination overseas, domestic opponents believe it exerts an irresistible control over its consumers. Conservative groups see media as the conveyor of moral depravity. On the liberal side, media is believed to transmit oppressive ideologies. Both views are unified by their belief that media must be resisted at all costs.[20] All of these arguments against the media share several common flaws: they assign a range of social problems to the media that originate elsewhere, and they make the incorrect assumption that representations invariably correspond to outcomes and that viewers exert no license in the viewing process.

Most importantly in the context of everyday culture, both conservative and liberal critiques of media emerge from a normative standpoint. In other words, both ends of the ideological spectrum share the belief that a single, correct perspective exists and that contemporary media diverts attention from it. This is not to suggest that there is any moral failing in preferring *Lost* over *Desperate Housewives*—or vice versa. But democracy begins to suffer when the rhetoric of preference reaches the point of suggesting that selected options should be discontinued, defunded, or censored. Crude as it sounds, this is exactly what groups such as Accuracy in Media, the American Family Association, and the Center for Media and Values often suggest.

In part, these antidemocratic sentiments stem from a lack of understanding about how media are received and interpreted. Hasty conclusions get drawn about the effects of media messages, with little consideration of the technical, institutional, and social contexts in which the communication transaction occurs. Instead, intellectuals, parents, and clergy make judgments about the media practices of the less powerful. This results in a condescending series of assumptions about the capabilities of viewers to evaluate what they see. Two common threads run through all of these claims against media: that viewers lack a capacity for subjective agency, and that media are inherently negative. The solutions to this perceived tyranny lie in turning off the tube or girding oneself to resist its mendacity. This has been the premise of media education, the rationale for the development of public broadcasting, and even the motivation for several United Nations resolutions. Obviously such beliefs don't give viewers very much credit. This perspective refuses to recognize that meaning develops in the relationship between text and reader, with readers actively comparing narratives to their own experiences. This position fails to consider the many ways that meaning is altered in the mechanics of information delivery. It also neglects to acknowledge viewers' abilities to accept portions of a text while discarding the rest. In short, this negative view of media insists that audiences are incapable of telling the difference between images and life itself.

Improvised Culture

Culture isn't something that people simply receive. And it doesn't exert an uncontrollable influence. There simply are too many different kinds of information buzzing around and competing for our attention. People have the option of choosing what they want to see and believe. They have the critical capabilities of rejecting what they don't like or what doesn't seem to have relevance. Different people bring different comprehensions, tastes, desires, and needs to every cultural encounter. Individuals emerge from different backgrounds with different kinds and amounts of education, and they have different aspirations and goals for the future.

Most importantly, received culture can't account for new situations that people encounter. A friend illustrated this to me with a story about the San Francisco Municiple Railway (Muni), the above- and below-ground rail system that covers much of the city. One warm summer day on the ride home, the train stopped. At first, people in the crowded car did what they normally do. They ignored each other. Minutes passed, and the air began to warm up. But the passengers' cultural understandings of what to do on the train kept them from talking or looking at each other. As more time passed, people began to fidget and to venture quiet complaints to each other. Eventually, the silence was broken with discussion about what to do, and a couple of people ventured to the front of the train to talk to the conductor. In breaking with convention, then talking, and finally acting upon the situation, the Muni riders created a new cultural moment. They improvised, formed a group, and took action. This is what makes culture interesting. The past is not always a guide for the future. The existing relationships among the Muni riders only went so far in telling them what to do. Then they had to make up something. At that moment, they demonstrated an important kind of freedom from tradition and past experience. This kind of improvisation presents itself to each of us every day. It invites us to make our own decisions and break free of the past. It's part of what gives everyday culture its dynamism and vitality.

But as culture becomes less fixed and overdetermined, it also becomes less stable. Despite the freedom and unpredictability that emerges from our everyday encounters with culture, there is nothing to guarantee that the experiences will be positive or beneficial. As Michel de Certeau observed, people's natural instincts or inherent tools for engaging with things like movies or TV programs don't necessarily cause them to do anything progressive with the meanings they derive or the conclusions they draw. Insight is required to help people become truly critical viewers and consumers—an insight that emerges from asking the right questions.

Introducing Cultural Studies

Cultural studies is one source of these questions. As an emerging field of study, cultural studies investigates the lack of consideration of everyday culture in existing academic disciplines and the negative ways the everyday is viewed in other schools of thought. The discipline especially takes issue with the way Marxism views consumerism. Historically, in Western societies the study of everyday culture was limited to what anthropologists did when they examined distant peoples in faraway lands. Little value was seen in studying the everyday consumer practices and aesthetic preferences of ordinary people, except in Marxist circles where mass culture was considered a manifestation of capitalist exploitation. In this pessimistic view, culture was perceived as little more than an advertisement for materialistic values and thus directly reflected the manipulative interests of the market. Frankfurt School scholars Max Horkheimer and Theodor Adorno, among others, described a system in which the masses were systematically duped into lives of servitude and consumption.[21] Within such apocalyptic logic, cultural objects functioned as propaganda, and the citizenry was incapable of resisting the seduction of the dominant "culture industry." Although useful in the broad mapping of ideological reproduction, such generalizations refused to grant consumers or audiences any autonomy whatsoever. Unabashedly elitist in its views of "the masses," the resulting "reflection theory" readings of culture invariably produced predictable evidence of existing class inequities.

Alternatives to reflection theory date to the 1940s, although until recently many were not widely discussed. Some of these alternative views emphasized the independent character of cultural works, apart from the presumed meanings they were thought to convey. Others focused on audiences. Louis Althusser's work, in particular, sought to undo myths of a direct correspondence between messages and their effects. In Althusser's essay "Ideology and Ideological State Apparatuses (Notes Toward an Investigation)," he argued that meanings occur in gaps between senders and receivers of information. Oppressive institutions create imaginary narratives about the "real" circumstances of peoples' lives. But these fictions often can be recognized as such.

In this way, Althusser proposed a revision of reflection theory that assigned a quasi-autonomy to audiences. No longer the helpless receivers of ideological messages, people were seen to operate in a complex dialectic with culture. In other words, a space was acknowledged between oppressive institutions and the consciousness of individuals. Within this space, resistances could form that were capable of destabilizing ruling power structures. These sentiments were echoed in the writings of Herbert Marcuse, who likewise argued against the classical Marxist doctrine that propaganda alone was responsible for producing consciousness. Emphasizing the role of human agency, Marcuse said that "radical change in consciousness is the beginning, the first step in changing social existence: emergence of the new Subject."[22]

A similar refinement of Marxist cultural theory came in 1970 when Hans Magnus Enzenberger proposed in his "Constituents of a Theory of Media" that communications experts had been misguided in their understandings of how culture operates. He suggested that instead of tricking the masses into a web of false wants, media actually found ways of satisfying real (but often unconscious) desires. This position was later elaborated upon by poststructuralist Marxists like Frederic Jameson and Roland Barthes, who further considered the negotiable possibilities of signification.[23] If cultural signs could be interpreted variously, their meanings assumed a "floating" character as individuals assigned them different readings. From these understandings of the contingency of meaning has evolved a complex discourse on a wide variety of factors that come into play as people interpret messages. The act of interpretation can be enhanced with study or critical intention.

Partly related to this Marxist history, cultural studies developed in Great Britain among intellectuals who wanted to study the British working class in the 1950s and who were concerned about the influx of post-war American culture into Britain. Early works in this regard were Raymond Williams's *The Long Revolution* (1961), which explored the relationships between culture and social habits, and Richard Hoggart's *The Uses of Literacy* (1958), that looked at working-class interests in sports, pubs, and similar sites of social interaction.[24] These inquiries became institutionalized in 1964 with the founding of the Center for Contemporary Cultural Studies (CCCS) in Birmingham, Great Britain. The center's research orientation toward working-class culture defined its interests in terms of topics largely excluded from traditional academic disciplines. Rather than focusing on established literary canons of acknowledged masterworks or the histories of great moments of the nation's past, cultural studies examined such "contemporary" topics as popular music, clubs, clothing, consumer habits, life at work or collecting welfare, and the dating practices of young adults. These research interests formed the bases for courses on the same topics of everyday culture, which proved of greater interest and relevance to students. Cultural studies courses, especially, appealed to students attending the British "polytechnic" colleges that, like community colleges in the United States, often served older and nontraditional students or simply those whose economic circumstances required them to hold jobs while attending school.

Students found the instruction useful because the courses addressed issues in their daily experience, like how they might become critical consumers, how they might become more effective in their jobs, more aware of the role media plays in their lives, or more cognizant of sexism, racism, or economic class relations in their everyday encounters. In this way, instruction at the CCCS had more than an abstract academic appeal. It provided tools for living and succeeding in the world. As stated by Stuart Hall, one of the early directors at Birmingham, a central goal was to "enable people to understand what was going on, and especially to provide ways of thinking, strategies for survival, and resources for resistance."[25]

Interdisciplinarity was the centerpiece of cultural studies theory. This interdisciplinarity emerged from the conviction that the traditional disciplines of English, mathematics, history, and science had once been important in dividing knowledge into coherent categories, but over time those categories had become mired in their own traditions and unresponsive to the changing world around them. Traditional literature nearly always talked about writings by men—just as art, music, and theater primarily excluded works by women. History placed Western civilization at its center, as did most accounts of science, mathematics, politics, and economics. Little attention was afforded in photography, publishing, film, and television, which traditionally had brought people the most information about themselves and the rest of the world. Writing and other forms of communication were important to cultural studies due to the function of language in maintaining cultural norms. As Trinh T. Minh-Ha states, "Where does language start, where does it end? In a way, no political reflection can dispense with a reflection of language."[26] In addressing the huge volume of ideas unaddressed by conventional disciplines, cultural studies was soon flanked by related new fields in women's' studies, ethnic studies, media studies, lesbian/gay studies, and other "area" studies. The impetus for these new academic fields emerged as many disenfranchised groups were similarly reacting against exclusionary practices in employment, government, and institutions of all kinds.

This had profound implications both inside and outside colleges and universities. For one thing, it challenged established hierarchies of "experts" and "specialists" who had for so long held a monopoly on what was considered important and what counted as "official" knowledge. It also called into question all forms of established authority and power. But the proponents of cultural studies wanted to be careful that their efforts didn't simply topple old institutions, only to be replaced by new ones. Hall and others wrote that cultural studies must always keep questioning its own premises and always keep changing in response to new circumstances. "Cultural studies is not one thing," Hall wrote, "it has never been one thing."[27] It should remain a dynamic affair, encompassing a variety of traditions and practices. As stated by Lawrence Grossberg, Cary Nelson, and Paul Treichler,

> Cultural studies remains a diverse and contentious enterprise, encompassing different positions and trajectories in specific contexts, addressing many questions, drawing nourishment from multiple roots, and shaping itself within different institutions and locations. The passage of time, encounters with new historical events, and the very extensions of cultural studies into

new disciplines and national contexts will inevitably change its meaning and uses. Cultural studies needs to remain open to unexpected, unimagined, and even uninvited possibilities. No one can hope to control these developments.[28]

Seen in its fullest terms, cultural studies has been described as incorporating "the history of cultural studies, gender and sexuality, nationhood and national identity, colonialism and postcolonialism, race and ethnicity, popular culture and its audiences, science and ecology, identity politics, pedagogy, the politics of aesthetics, cultural institutions, the politics of disciplinarity, discourse and textuality, history, global culture in a postmodern age."[29]

But Is It Art?

Art has a peculiar history in Western society, which has produced narrow and mystified perceptions in the minds of many people about what art is. People often see art as something rare and special, which is only produced by professional artists or people with extraordinary natural skill. This view of art excludes artwork by hobbyists, amateurs, children, or anyone else not deemed capable of making fine art. But this exclusionary view does little to explain what fine art does or why it is so special. Instead, the aesthetic and social aspects are obscured and mystified. This leaves many average citizens with the suspicion that art—especially modern and conceptual art—is little more than a hoax or some kind of money-making scheme. Of course, art doesn't exist in a vacuum. It is created by a variety of people in different vocations and supported by numerous kinds of institutions. Art schools and colleges are part of a system that trains, evaluates, and accredits artists as professionals. Occasionally, art institutions will exhibit work by folk artists or so-called primitives who exhibit an unusual style or manifest a particular cultural or historical uniqueness. But often the difference between art made by artists and nonartists is difficult for viewers to discern. This is especially the case with certain kinds of twentieth-century art intentionally produced by artists to confuse or call into question the conventions by which value is conferred on artworks by institutions. One famous instance of this occurred when Frenchman Marcel Duchamp brought industrially fabricated objects like plumbing fixtures into the art gallery and proclaimed they were are art because they were labeled as such when put on display.

All of this can leave the average person quite confused, as is manifest in surveys conducted about public perceptions of art. When asked about the general value of art to society, eighty-nine percent of people in the United States say that art is "important to the growth and development of their communities."[30] This is even more the case with parents, ninety-six percent of whom believe that art education should be a part every child's school curriculum.[31] But things change dramatically when people are asked about their own relationship with art.[32] Only six percent report that they ever engaged in art making.[33] Four percent report that they volunteer at art museums.[34] According to the National Endowment for the Arts, more than three-quarters of the population fails to enter a museum even once per year.[35] Although people strongly support high culture and fine art as abstract ideas, these things appear to have little role in people's daily lives.

In large part, this alienation from fine art comes from the way art is presented to people by most art institutions and in many educational settings. Art is presented as something guarded during the day, locked up at night, available in particular places, and not produced by ordinary people. Artists, art galleries, museums, schools, critics, and publications all work together within an economic system throughout the Western world to maintain art as a scarce and valuable commodity. The community an artist addresses is fundamentally a clientele that uses (or purchases) professional expertise. Edward Said has pointed out that as this role is accepted by artists, what they do can become neutralized and nonpolitical. This creates an ethic of specialization that encourages practitioners to minimize the content of their work and increase the "composite wall of guild consciousness, social authority, and exclusionary discipline around themselves. Opponents are therefore not people in disagreement with the constituency but people to be kept out, non-experts and non-specialists, for the most part."[36] This exclusion extends to amateurs, students, eccentric practitioners, and anyone without some form of institutional validation.

The entire enterprise hinges on art defined by strict characteristics and representing selected philosophical ideals. Some social critics point out that the Western notion of art is a relatively recent phenomenon, evolving in the past two hundred years, following a prior more utilitarian and practical view of art in the West in the pre-Renaissance period.[37] In Europe during the Middle Ages (500 A.D. through the fourteenth century), art was viewed as a commodity made by craftspeople. Visual art was produced by people hired to decorate public places and the dwellings of sponsors. Performing artists likewise produced street theater or entertainment on commission. Art was viewed as an entertaining substance that was accessible to the aristocrat and common person alike.

Both perception and the support of art changed in the Renaissance period (fourteenth to seventeenth centuries). With the development of what was termed *idealist* philosophy came beliefs that certain ideas existed beyond the realm of ordinary people and were matters for gifted individuals. Art carried with it an aura or specialness that only "genius" could provide. As such, art also took on an added value beyond its mere material worth. This change in the way art was valued paralleled the emergence of markets and international trade, when commodities were bought and sold not merely for their exchange value, but with cost added according to the availability or scarceness of the products.

With the industrial era (eighteenth and nineteenth centuries), the idealization of art became more powerful. Artists were seen as quasi-magical people, alienated from society and empowered with special gifts of talent. Art became valued more for its scarcity than its intrinsic worth. During this period, the nature of skilled work was altered by the emergence of the machine, the factory, and the assembly line. For example, the artful aspect of making a shoe by hand was replaced by the mechanical manufacturing of shoes. Creative satisfaction was no longer derived from work, but became something one might encounter at the end of the day or on a special occasion.

The twentieth century brought the full-blown institutionalization of art—with the rise of art museums and commercial art galleries. In the United States, changes in federal tax codes allowed a new class of wealthy industrialists to gain tax benefits through philanthropy and the establishment of private foundations.[38] Frederick H. Goff created the first community foundation in Cleveland, Ohio. Community foundations were not designed to help people directly, but were seen as instruments of reform, which could address the root causes of poverty, hunger, and disease. In the early 1900s, civic and business leaders Andrew Carnegie, John Rockefeller, and Margaret Olivia Sage used the foundation model to organize philanthropic endeavors, like the business corporations they had built so successfully. This business-oriented structure permitted more flexibility than charitable trusts, which had been the traditional mode of giving featured in English law. Corporate foundations came later, after the concept of direct giving by businesses was resolved under United States law in 1935. Corporate foundations grew at a rapid rate during the 1940s, an era of high profits and high tax levels. This created a climate for the growth of an entire sector of nonprofit organizations.

Meanwhile, popular perceptions of art and artists continued to change. With the emergence of avant-garde movements in Europe and the United States, public attitudes placed artists even further from the social mainstream. Artists were regarded as visionaries or eccentrics, motivated by muses, ideological extremism, or driven by insanity. As mechanical reproduction and the development of photography made it possible for anyone to own a copy of a famous artwork, the scarcity of original artworks became the rationale for valuation. If an artist's work was deemed exceptional by experts or curators, and the availability of the artist's work was in short supply, then the monetary value of the artwork would rise. Thus, the prices of work by dead artists quickly began to exceed that of living producers who might continue to create works for the market. The twentieth century also witnessed the increased use of art by governments to boast their nation's superiority. Following World War II, the United States emerged as a world superpower and proclaimed American abstract expressionism the leading art movement of its day.

The hyperbolic growth of the art marketplace and the view of fine art as a commodity haven't done much to clarify popular understandings of what art is. A quick look at the way terms like "art" and "artwork" are defined in leading dictionaries is instructive. The *Oxford English Dictionary* defines *art* as "the expression of creative skill through a visual medium such as painting or sculpture" and a *work of art* as "a creative product with strong imaginative or aesthetic appeal."[39] The *Merriam-Webster's Dictionary* defines a *work of art* as either "the product of one of the arts; especially: a painting or sculpture of high aesthetic quality" or "something giving high aesthetic satisfaction to the viewer or listener."[40] These notions of art as either skillful aptitude or aesthetic creativity do little to demystify the actual functions of art in society. In his book *Definitions of Art,* Stephen Davies takes a considerably broader and more socially inclusive view in asserting that three general theories describe art:

Functionalism: Art is defined by purpose(s) that make art useful or valuable. A function commonly assigned to art is to provide a satisfying aesthetic experience. Art can also stimulate innovation, tell stories, teach moral lessons, bear witness to history, convey humor or lust, evoke social concern or political activism, or simply comment on art itself.

Proceduralism: Art achieves its status through specific processes and social contexts. Some of these include academic certification by historians and museum curators, economic valuation by art galleries and collectors, peer acknowledgment by other artists, acclaim from critics and the media, educational endorsement by schools and teachers. The acceptance and belief of the viewing public in the importance of art also is a form of proceduralism.

Historicism: The concept of art is itself evolving, and art status requires appropriate connections to previous art and art movements. So what is art at one time will not be art at another time. Contemporary art frequently is evaluated according to the extent that it either extends or breaks with historical tradition. Art history organizes the study of art from the past and often conveys value on art in doing so.[41]

While the categories put forward by Davies provide more specificity to the definition of art, they still operate largely in the idealist tradition of art separated from contemporary everyday culture. Such nonutilitarian forms of expression are sometimes identified with "fine art" to distinguish them from creative trades of the mass-produced culture of "applied art." These correspond to the categories of high and low culture discussed earlier.

One can break through the obfuscation of the fine/applied art divide by examining art in vocational terms. Doing so reveals a complexity in the role of art in contemporary society that belies the idealist ethos that so dominates most discussions of art and that confounds public understanding of the role of art in everyday life. The U.S. Department of Labor's Bureau of Labor Statistics (BLS) divides artists into four categories: "*Art directors* formulate design concepts and presentation approaches for visual communications media. *Craft artists* create or reproduce handmade objects for sale or exhibition. *Multimedia artists and animators* create special effects, animation, or other visual images on film, on video, or with computers or other electronic media. *Fine artists,* including *painters, sculptors, and illustrators* create original artwork, using a variety of media and techniques."[42] This is how the BLS describes these vocational categories:

Art directors develop design concepts and review material that is to appear in periodicals, newspapers, and other printed or digital media. They decide how best to present the information visually, so that it is eye-catching, appealing, and organized. Art directors decide which photographs or artwork to use and oversee the layout design and production of the printed material. They may direct workers engaged in artwork, layout design, and copywriting.

Craft artists hand make a wide variety of objects that are sold either in their own studios, in retail outlets, or at arts and crafts shows. Some craft artists may display their works in galleries and museums. Craft artists work with many different materials—ceramics, glass, textiles, wood, metal, and paper—to create unique pieces of art, such as pottery, stained glass, quilts, tapestries, lace, candles, and clothing. Many craft artists also use fine art techniques—for example, painting, sketching, and printing—to add finishing touches to their art.

Multimedia artists and animators work primarily in motion picture and video industries, advertising, and computer systems design services. They draw by hand and use computers to create the large series of pictures that form the animated images or special effects seen in movies, television programs, and computer games. Some draw storyboards for television commercials, movies, and animated features. Storyboards present television commercials in a series of scenes similar to a comic strip and allow an advertising agency to evaluate commercials proposed by the company doing the advertising. Storyboards also serve as guides to placing actors and cameras on the television or motion picture set and to other details that need to be taken care of during the production of commercials.

Fine artists typically display their work in museums, commercial art galleries, corporate collections, and private homes. Some of their artwork may be commissioned (done on request from clients), but most is sold by the artist or through private art galleries or dealers. The gallery and the artist predetermine how much each will earn from the sale. Only the most successful fine artists are able to support themselves solely through the sale of their works. Most fine artists have at least one other job to support their art careers. Some work in museums or art galleries as fine arts directors or as curators, planning and setting up art exhibits. A few artists work as art critics for newspapers or magazines or as consultants to foundations or institutional collectors. Other artists teach art classes or conduct workshops in schools or in their own studios. Some artists also hold full-time or part-time jobs unrelated to the art field and pursue fine art as a hobby or second career.[43]

In an effort to sort out the complexities, overlapping categories, and combined forms of practice, the BLS defines fine artists as producers of "original works." Although the BLS categories hardly exhaust the variety of art practitioners and practices, they begin to demonstrate that art can have many definitions and serve many functions beyond the constrained view of art that has evolved in the popular mind of the West over the past five hundred years.

Work by artists infuses nearly every aspect of contemporary life. Art institutions create jobs, entertainment, tourism, and an art market. In 2006–2007, more than seventeen thousand museums existed in the United States alone, accounting for billions of dollars in collections holdings and serving huge international audiences. Television, film, interactive media, and the performing arts inform and move billions of people worldwide, making up important industries and export/import markets. Artists help connect form with function in fashioning everything from homes and automobiles to consumer goods and expendable commodities. Effective graphic design and use of visual language are essential in effective communication of content to readers, viewers, and audiences in general. Art is significant in certain forms of psychological treatment and in occupational therapy, as well as a diagnostic tool for psychiatrists and other mental health professions.

Many people credit art with contributing to a healthy working or living environment. Art is an important element in advertising, public relations, packaging, and product design. Artistic qualities can influence how consumers respond to products, what they buy, and how they use items ranging from clothing to home appliances. Art is a tool used by educators to teach language, history, religion, social science, and many other subjects. It conveys content for some subjects and alternative pedagogies for others. For many people, art conveys transcendent philosophical ideals or is used to dramatize theological lessons and values. Art has been credited with inspiring love, compassion, empathy, ethnic and national pride, ethnic tolerance, as well as prejudice and hatred. In many communities, art activities such as clubs, classes, after-school programs, and exhibitions contribute to civic health and to people's sense of belonging. Artists can serve as role models and can involve young people and others in art activities. Art can be a way of communicating democratic ideas. The display of art in public institutions can be a way of informing a community, encouraging a population to participate in collective activities or stimulating engagement. As this listing of art's functions is meant to suggest, the meaning of the term "art" is largely determined by use and context. Art is a dynamic idea, which is limited and misunderstood when narrowly categorized as is often done in fine art or high cultural contexts.[44]

What Everybody Wants

Just as art can be found in nearly every aspect of contemporary culture, many of the things that ordinary people do can be considered artistic. People make creative decisions every day from the minute they get up in the morning and decide what to wear. Unacknowledged aesthetic decisions inform such everyday activities as preparing food, shopping at the mall, decorating one's room, tending a garden, or choosing a TV program. These artistic decisions in everyday life derive from the artist that lives inside each person—the artist that has been repressed by a society that teaches us that art is made only by the few, the talented, or the lucky. In reality, art is something that everyone does. Art describes who we are, and it helps us communicate with each other.

How does this process of everyday creativity work? Many people derive a sense of identity from the media and entertainment they consume, as well as a pleasure in buying things as a way of expressing themselves. To some, consumer choice represents a use of a skill or an application of knowledge in the interest of efficiency, economy, or self-advancement. To others, consumption can serve as an antidote to feelings of powerlessness and alienation from big government, large corporations, and other institutions that exert power over them. The pleasure one gets from the organization of one's material possessions provides an expressive outlet that many of us take for granted. Selecting a CD or a car affords a reassurance in expressing one's identity by taking a degree of control over the immediate world. Cultural theorist Paul Willis has written extensively about the expressive potential in the everyday pursuits of consumer behavior.[45] To Willis, the "symbolic creativity" found in these mundane activities plays a central role in the way we engage with the world, make sense of it through our interrelations, and stake out a territory we can call our own. Willis writes, "Symbolic work and creativity mediate, and are simultaneously expanded and developed by, the uses, meanings, and effects of cultural commodities. Cultural commodities are catalyst, not product; a stage in, not the destination of, cultural affairs. Consumerism now has to be understood as an active, not passive, process."[46] Willis sees people's creative consumerism operating in opposition to a high cultural sphere he believes excludes most people. According to Willis,

> The institutions and practices, genres and terms of high art are
> currently categories of exclusions more than inclusions. They

have no real connection to most people or their lives. They may encourage some artistic specializations, but they certainly discourage much wider and more general symbolic creativity. The official existence of arts in institutions seems to exhaust everything else of its artistic content. If some things count as "art," the rest must be "nonart." Because "art" is in the "art gallery," it can't therefore be anywhere else.[47]

According to Willis, young people in particular establish a sense of identity by their acts of everyday creativity and consumer choice. He gives consumers a great deal of credit for being able to outsmart advertisers and retailers who work to manipulate taste and control buying habits. In many ways, Willis's formulation of symbolic creativity parallels the beliefs most people hold about the market. Burger King, Pepsi, and The Gap may make convincing arguments about why you should buy their products, but at the end of the day each of us makes our own decisions.

For all of its commonsense appeal, Willis's formulation has a number of flaws. The most obvious lies in the way it generalizes the workings of popular culture and high art. Consumption and the choice of a drink or a pair of jeans may allow people a degree of autonomy some of the time, but just as often consumers are responding to a promotional pitch they've heard. Michel de Certeau, among others, has commented about the indeterminacy of spectatorship and consumerism.[48] Individuals exert a degree of control over what they see and how they interpret it. They exercise some autonomy over what they buy and do with the goods they consume. But this control and autonomy is partial, at best—and not necessarily progressive or even self-serving. As de Certeau writes, before we get too carried away with optimistic assumptions, any discussion of the way viewers derive pleasure in "the images broadcast by television (representation) and the time spent watching television (behavior) should be complimented by a study of what the consumer 'makes' or 'does' during this time and with these images. The same goes for the use of urban space, the products purchased in the supermarket, the stories and legends distributed by the newspapers, and so on."[49]

Popular Culture and Capitalism

So which is it? Do people exercise autonomy and free will in their consumer behavior, or are they tricked and controlled by the marketplace? After all, despite the choice and creativity that people exhibit in their consuming and viewing practices, aren't popular attitudes largely shaped by the marketplace? Consumers may express themselves by the clothes they wear and the cars they drive, but most of the ideas and values they associate with those commodities generally come from the commercial sphere. Or do they? Can it really be concluded that the very image of a "self" that many people believe they are assembling by accumulating and displaying consumer goods is made up of images they have gotten from advertising? This raises the possibility that perhaps this image-constructed self—received from Old Navy, Nike, Puma, Guess, Banana Republic, Abercrombie and Fitch, Ralph Lauren, and Victoria's Secret, to name a few—is really an illusion. Could it be that the thing we call the self actually is little more than a selection of images that we have been sold?

The answer is yes and no. On one hand, it might be argued that the presumed freedom we experience in selecting what we buy is really little more than an illusion of choice. The commercial marketplace has already chosen the array of goods available to us. It then simply lets us "choose" from what it has made available. On the other hand, one might argue that all of life already is a set of choices from what is available. Although we may be constructing our self from advertising images, it is a creative process nevertheless. Some postmodern theorists have asserted that there really is no such thing as an "authentic" self or even an authentic reality.[50] All of the moments we experience are really little more than representations of a world because each of us understands those moments differently. Choosing a number of advertising images to represent us is just as creative and individual an act as naïvely believing we can experience reality.

Many people blame television for the dramatic influence that advertising exerts over us. Americans own more television sets than any other nation—nearly one set per person.[51] As Juliet B. Schor wrote in *Born to Buy,* "Heavy viewing has resulted in historically unprecedented exposure to commercials. And ads have proliferated far beyond the television screen to virtually every social institution and type of public space, from museums and zoos, to college campuses and elementary school classrooms, restaurant bathrooms and menus, at the airport, even in the sky."[52]

It is important to stress that commercials alone do not make people buy things. Most people begin to establish purchasing habits in the context of their family upbringing, learning consumer behavior as they grow up. Along the way, many of us develop a powerful drive to keep up with the consuming habits of friends, neighbors, coworkers, and other students. There exists a strong social pressure to maintain levels of appearance and to achieve certain visible standards of living.

All of this contributes to a frequent confusion that people experience between the basic goods required for survival and comfort and the unnecessary commodities that people think they should have. Schor describes this as a confusion between what she terms "needs" and "wants." The fundamental items that people "need" are rather basic: food, clothing, shelter, and transportation. But most people are not content with minimally satisfying these needs. Instead, a desire grows based on "wants": gourmet food, designer clothing, a larger apartment, a fancy car. Schor stresses the fundamental distinction between what people need and what they want: "In the not very distant past, this dichotomy was not only well understood, but the basis of data collection and social policy. Need was a social concept with real force. All that's left now is an economy of desire."[53] Schor adds, "This is reflected in polling data. Just over forty percent of adults earning $50,000 to $100,000 a year, and twenty-seven percent of those earning more than $100,000, agree that 'I cannot afford to buy everything I really need.'" [54]One-third of the first group and nineteen percent of those earning more than $100,000 say that they spend all of their money on the basic necessities of life.[55]

Consumption and Ideology

For decades, theorists argued that people get persuaded to desire certain things or behave in certain ways by unscrupulous advertisers and promoters. In other words, theorists believe society is driven by a huge propaganda system.[56] But that doesn't give people much credit for independent thinking, and it assumes that people's only real desires are those they are tricked into having. More recently, a new set of theories has come along that looks at the situation slightly differently. Perhaps ideology doesn't give people new ideas about what they want but instead caters to things people really value—like love, friendship, and safety—and convinces them that they can only get these things by behaving in certain ways or by buying the right things.[57] This is the real genius of modern capitalism. It's gotten people to believe that the road to happiness lies in material possessions and superficial signs of success. This process of ideology is what makes the consuming part of identity work. You think you need to have the right car or the right clothes to look good and be admired. And who doesn't want to look good and be admired? There's nothing really wrong with it.

How did consumer demand for purchases get so out of control? Schor cites what she terms the escalating "work and speed" cycle. The American work week has expanded at the same time that public demand for commodities has also grown. People work harder and longer and they want more for their efforts. The cruel part of contemporary marketing is that it tells you that if you can't afford to buy those things you're out of luck. And it doesn't stop with small things. Looking good evolved over time in response to the dominant groups in Western society and what those groups thought was important. In the United States and Britain as well as much of Europe this meant good looks were determined by white- or light-skinned people in societies governed by men—heterosexual men. If you look through fashion magazines—or any magazines for that matter—you'll see ads promoting a certain kind of beauty. It's a beauty of thin, clear-skinned, young white women with enough money to buy clothes and makeup and great hair. It's a beauty that leaves out anyone with a black or brown complexion, as well as any woman who is big or poor or over thirty. In this way, the message sent out by the contemporary beauty and fashion industry is racist, classist, ageist, and degrading to anyone who doesn't fit its profile. And most women don't fit its profile.

Occasional efforts are made in the media industries to reverse these trends. *Marie Claire* editor Liz Jones attempted in 2000 to launch initiatives to encourage magazine editors to feature a wider diversity of women, specifically calling for models of different physical proportions and more African American and Asian American women. Her efforts were rejected by the industry and Jones resigned from the magazine in 2001, stating "I had simply had enough of working in an industry that pretends to support women while it bombards them with impossible images of perfection day after day, undermining their self-confidence, their health, their hard-earned cash."[58]

The same basic set of rules applies to men. But here behavior matters as well as looks. Men are told that they need to look right. But with a man the emphasis is placed a little more on having an impressive car and other things that show he has enough money or is smart enough to get it. But media images of men often say that they have to be tough in certain ways as well. Here, violence enters the picture. Many contemporary television shows, movies, and video games tell a man he needs to be able to use force, to fight when necessary, and that fighting is a suitable way to solve problems or acquire things in certain situations. This is one way that media violence really does shape people's thinking. It works in the background, in our subconscious minds, making subtle changes in our attitudes about the world and how we behave. Of course, there is a broader context that helps media violence accomplish this. TV shows, movies, and games are by no means the whole story.

The effects of stereotypes and media violence are never absolute. Critically minded viewers continually question and contest what they see. And even the most regressive programming can contain positive elements. Lara Croft may be a hypersexualized, cartoonlike image of unattainable physical proportions, but she also represents strength, courage, and ethical responsibility in the eyes of her fans. As David Gauntlett writes, "Rather than being the object of desire who inspires the hero to action, Lara Croft is the hero, driving the story forward on her own, and reserving the right to eye certain men with desire."[59]

Attitudes toward Consumer Culture

Sorting out the complex and at times contradictory perspectives and theoretical approaches to mass media and consumer culture can be daunting. The three broad categories described below—*Celebration, Condemnation,* and *Critical Use*—draw together arguments from major viewpoints on various sides of the debates on these issues.

Celebration. The celebration view exalts the benefits of capitalism and the marketplace. It views consumer culture as a nonpolitical and humanistic enterprise characterized by a *freedom of choice.* The celebration view derives from the assumption that people are rational in their buying decisions and that they act in their own best interests. Juliet Schor describes this view as the "consumer knows best" perspective.[60] The celebration model also assumes that the marketplace *reflects real social needs.* The market satisfies the natural desires of the consumers who are regarded as well-informed, knowledgeable about products, and in possession of accurate information about what they are buying. The entire consumption process is *nondiscriminatory* because it accurately responds to people's real needs without prejudice or inherent elitism. People make their buying choices as independent individuals and these decisions have no secondary effects on other people. The consuming process is *nonpolitical* because it is neutral in value and because alternatives to the market exist and are freely available. Within the celebration view arguments are often made that people can patronize as they choose, shop elsewhere, or change the TV channel as expressions of their consumer freedom.

Condemnation. The condemnation view sees consumer culture as an expression of false consciousness. *No freedom of choice* exists because the overall range of existing choices is predetermined. A store may offer what appears to be a selection of twenty brands of deodorant, but the selection of the brands has already been made by the merchandiser. The issue of freedom of choice is further problematic because some consumers do not act in their own best interest and at times make choices based on poor judgment or incomplete information. These poor decisions result from a system of marketing and advertising that *promotes false consciousness* by distorting needs and instilling irrational desires. The condemnation approach was promoted by theorists of the Austrian Frankfurt School in the 1930s, including Theodor Adorno and Max Horkheimer. This negative view of consuming was also a popular theme of the New Left among such U.S. intellectuals as John Kenneth Galbraith, who asserted that people had been manipulated by an anti-intellectual culture of mass-produced entertainment and selfish values. Consumer culture was seen as inherently *discriminatory* because it promoted unattainable levels of material accumulation and standards of appearance that are presented as natural and unchangeable. Condemnation sees consumption as *politically biased* because it is often driven by competition, self-interest, and values of inequality.

Critical Use. The critical use view is well-summarized by what Schor terms the "New Politics of Consumption."[61] Consumers exercise the ability to *accept, reject, or change* when confronted with buying options. The ultimate criterion in making purchasing decisions shifts to determining what promotes a better standard of living—rather than the appearance of elevated status. Free *choice is both present and contested* as consumers decide whether to accept what is available or look elsewhere for what they want. Needs are seen as neither exclusively true or false. Emphasis is placed on the "quality of life rather than the quantity of stuff."[62] The critical use model *confronts discrimination* by recognizing that some goods are not available to all people and that certain consuming practices are destructive both to people and to the environment. Critical use is *politically informed* in the ways it addresses inequities in the availability of commodities and recognizes that some consuming practices promote social inequality by valuing luxury, scarcity, unavailability, and by working against resource management and environmental well-being.

These discussions of everyday culture, art, and consumption can leave one somewhat depressed—or at the very least perplexed. With so many forces exerting pressure on what we do and how we perceive the world, can any enjoyment remain in the simple routines of communication and consumption that make up so much of everyday living? The answer is yes. After all, one can't disengage from our market-oriented society, even if one wants to do so. One can only make the best of it with critical decisions. But a posture of criticality can only be maintained part of the time. One of the tricky workings of ideology is its unconscious side. In my conscious mind I may know that advertising and stylistic convention may be seducing me to want that new pair of shoes. But something deeper makes me desire them anyway. The best I can do is negotiate the dialectic of critical awareness and unconscious desire because they both define who I am. A person who lives in either of those worlds is only half a person.

Notes

1. Raymond Williams, "Culture and Society," (1958) in *Resources of Hope: Culture, Democracy, Socialism* (New York and London: Verso, 1989), 10.

2. William Henry III, *In Defense of Elitism* (New York: Anchor, 1995).

3. Howard Becker, *Doing Things Together* (Chicago: Northwestern University Press, 1986), 24.

4. Pierre Bourdieu, *Distinction: A Social Critique of the Judgment of Taste* (Cambridge, Mass.: Harvard University Press, 1984).

5. Ibid.

6. Alexis de Tocqueville, *Democracy in America* (1835; reprint, New York: Schocken Books, 1961).

7. Allan Bloom, *The Closing of the American Mind* (New York: Simon and Schuster, 1987); and E. D. Hirsch, Jr., *Cultural Literacy: What Every American Needs to Know* (Boston: Houghton Mifflin, 1987).

8. Bloom, 2.

9. de Tocqueville, *Democracy in America*, 309–310.

10. James Atlas, "The Battle of the Books," *New York Times Magazine*, June 5, 1988, 26.

11. "Santorum Marriage Plan Built on Strong Foundation of Gay Loathing," *Wonkett*, May 23, 2005. *http://www.wonkette.com/politics/culture-war/santorum-marriage-built-on-strong-foundation-of-gay-loathing-104616.php* Internet reference. Accessed May 3, 2006.

12. John Berger, *Ways of Seeing* (New York: Pelican, 1977) p. 52.

13. Ibid.

14. Laura Mulvey, "Visual Pleasure and Narrative Cinema," *Screen* 16, no. 3 (1975): 6–28.

15. Ibid., 27.

16. Benedict Anderson, *Imagined Communities: Reflections on the Origin and Spread of Nationalism*, revised edition (London and New York: Verso, 1991).

17. Ibid., p. 22.

18. Homi K. Bhabha, "DissemiNation: Time, Narrative, and the Margins of the Modern Nation," in Homi K. Bhabha, *Nation and Narration* (London and New York: Routledge, 1990), 2.

19. David Morley and Kevin Robins, "Spaces of Identity: Communications Technologies and the Refiguration of Europe," *Screen* 30, no. 4 (Autumn 1989): 12.

20. David Buckingham, "Teaching About the Media," in *The Media Studies Book*, ed. David Lusted (New York: Routledge, 1991), 12.

21. Max Horkheimer and Theodor Adorno, *The Dialectic of Enlightenment*, trans. John Cumming (New York: Herder and Herder, 1972).

22. Herbert Marcuse, *An Essay on Liberation* (Boston: Beacon Press, 1969), 21.

23. Fredric Jameson, *The Political Unconscious* (Ithaca: Cornell University Press, 1981); Roland Barthes, *Mythologies*, trans. Annette Lavers (New York: Hill and Wang, 1972).

24. Raymond Williams, *The Long Revolution* (New York: Columbia University Press, 1961); Richard Hoggart, *The Uses of Literacy* (New York: Penguin, 1958).

25. Lawrence Grossberg, Cary Nelson, and Paula Treichler, "Cultural Studies: An Introduction," in *Cultural Studies*, eds. Lawrence Grossberg, Cary Nelson, and Paula Treichler (New York: Routledge, 1992), 2.

26. Trinh T. Minh-Ha, *Framer Framed* (New York and London: Routledge, 1992), 252

27. Ibid., 3.

28. Ibid.

29. Ibid., 1.

30. Regional Art & Culture Council/Riley Research Associates, "The Value of Arts & Culture: A Public Opinion Survey," Spring 2005. *http://www.racc.org/resources/research/publicopinionsurvey.php#executiveoverview.* Accessed June 20, 2006.

31. Cultural Policy and the Arts National Data Archive (CPANDA), "Quick Facts About the Arts—Arts Education," 2002. *http://www.cpanda.org/arts-culture-facts/arts-ed.html.* Accessed June 20, 2006.

32. "Where People Get their News," Pew Center for People and the Press, May 7, 2005. *http://people-press.org/reports/display. php3?PageID=834.* Accessed June 20, 2005.

33. Bobbie Nichols, *Demographic Characteristics of Arts Attendance, 2002* (Washington, DC: National Endowment for the Arts).

34. Ibid.

35. Ibid.

36. Edward Said, "Opponents, Audiences, Constituencies and Community," in *The Anti-Aesthetic,* ed. Hal Foster (Port Townsend, Wash.: Bay Press), 152.

37. Janet Wolff, *The Social Production of Art* (New York: New York University Press, 1993).

38. Council on Foundations, *An Abbreviated History of the Philanthropic Tradition in the United States. http://www.cof.org/Action/content. cfm?ItemNumber=730.* Accessed June 21, 2006.

39. "AskOxford.com," *Oxford Dictionaries, http://www.askoxford. com/* Accessed Feb. 20, 2007.

40. "Merriam-Webster Online," *Merriam-Webster Dictionaries. http://www.m-w.com/* Accessed Feb. 20, 2007.

41. Stephen Davies, *Definitions of Art* (Ithaca: Cornell University Press, 1991).

42. Bureau of Labor Statistics (BLS), "Artists and Related Workers," *Occupational Outlook Handbook* (Washington, DC: U.S. Department of Labor, 2006). *http://www.bls.gov/oco/ocos092.htm.* Accessed Sept. 4, 2006.

43. Ibid. Within the designation of "fine artists," the BLS identified the following supplementary—and somewhat idiosyncratic—list of vocations. "*Illustrators* typically create pictures for books, magazines, and other publications and for commercial products such as textiles, wrapping paper, stationery, greeting cards, and calendars. Increasingly, illustrators are working in digital format, preparing work directly on a computer. *Medical* and *scientific illustrators* combine drawing skills with knowledge of biology or other sciences. Medical illustrators draw illustrations of human anatomy and surgical procedures. Scientific illustrators draw illustrations

of animal and plant life, atomic and molecular structures, and geologic and planetary formations. The illustrations are used in medical and scientific publications and in audiovisual presentations for teaching purposes. Medical illustrators also work for lawyers, producing exhibits for court cases. *Cartoonists* draw political, advertising, social, and sports cartoons. Some cartoonists work with others who create the idea or story and write the captions. Most cartoonists have comic, critical, or dramatic talents in addition to drawing skills. *Sketch artists* create likenesses of subjects with pencil, charcoal, or pastels. Sketches are used by law enforcement agencies to assist in identifying suspects, by the news media to depict courtroom scenes, and by individual patrons for their own enjoyment. *Sculptors* design three-dimensional artworks, either by molding and joining materials such as clay, glass, wire, plastic, fabric, or metal or by cutting and carving forms from a block of plaster, wood, or stone. Some sculptors combine various materials to create mixed-media installations. Some incorporate light, sound, and motion into their works. *Printmakers* create printed images from designs cut or etched into wood, stone, or metal. After creating the design, the artist inks the surface of the woodblock, stone, or plate and uses a printing press to roll the image onto paper or fabric. Some make prints by pressing the inked surface onto paper by hand or by graphically encoding and processing data, using a computer. The digitized images are then printed on paper with the use of a computer printer. *Painting restorers* preserve and restore damaged and faded paintings. They apply solvents and cleaning agents to clean the surfaces of the paintings, they reconstruct or retouch damaged areas, and they apply preservatives to protect the paintings. Restoration is highly detailed work and usually is reserved for experts in the field."

44. A further broadened listing of artistic functions and forms would include the following: Art gives people a voice, a way to express something with words or through symbolic explication. Art allows individuals to convey the intimacy of personal experience or to speak on behalf of groups, populations, or cultures. Art often offers new or unusual perspectives. Art asks questions and challenges traditional assumptions and beliefs. Corporations increasingly include artists in product development teams and seek

out artists for their abilities to "think outside the box" and work in quickly formed teams and collaborative groups. Artworks portray historical eras, events, and values. Art records the accomplishments of groups as well as the fates that have befallen them. Art keeps alive the specificity of human difference and past tradition.

45.　Paul Willis, *Common Culture: Symbolic Work at Play in the Everyday Cultures of the Young* (Boulder and San Francisco: Westview Press, 1992), 1.

46.　Ibid., 18.

47.　Ibid., 1.

48.　de Certeau, *The Practice of Everyday Life*.

49.　Ibid., xii.

50.　Juliet B. Schor, *Born To Buy* (New York: Scribner, 2004).

51.　Ibid., 9.

52.　Ibid.

53.　Juliet B. Schor, "Towards a New Politics of Consumption," in *The Consumer Society Reader,* eds. Juliet B. Schor and Douglas B. Holt (New York: The New Press, 2000), 459.

54.　Ibid.

55.　Ibid.

56.　Louis Althusser, "Ideology and Ideological State Apparatuses," in *Lenin and Philosophy and Other Essays* (New York: Monthly Review Press, 1971).

57.　Hans Magnus Enzenberger, *Critical Essays* (New York: Continuum, 1982).

58.　David Gauntlett, *Media, Gender, and Identity: An Introduction* (New York: Routledge, 2002), 195.

59.　Ibid., 39.

60.　Juliet B. Schor, "The New Politics of Consumption: Why Americans Want So Much More Than They Need," in *The Boston Review* (Summer 1999).

61.　Ibid.

62.　Ibid., 15.

CHAPTER THREE
READING

LANGUAGE, COMMUNICATION, AND NEW MEDIA

Reading takes place everywhere in all kinds of unexpected ways. Any discussion of everyday culture requires a discussion of the ways that ordinary people interpret the movies and TV they watch, the radio and music they listen to, the toys and games they play. In the broadest sense it can be said that people "read" the media in quite diverse ways, bringing to the interpretative encounter their various educational histories, cultural backgrounds, and levels of literacy, as well as their tastes, biases, and opinions. Forms of culture play out differently in different cultural activities—shopping, going to school, traveling, work, and leisure—as well as in different media. To a certain extent everyone possesses a degree of critical skill. It's often said that the TV generation has a level of media literacy superior to the print generations that preceded it. Today's digital generation is more media literate than its predecessors who grew up without computers or the Internet.

No one needs reminding that media—photography, video, film, the Internet, and interactive computer games—plays an enormous role in our lives. The U.S. Department of Labor estimates that the average adult spends four hours every day watching TV, two hours listening to the radio, thirty minutes online, and thirty minutes reading.[1] Regardless of one's viewing habits or the time one spends at any one media activity, it's hard to deny the importance of media culture in shaping our understandings of who we are and how we got here. So accustomed have we become to using media for learning about those around us, our communities, national, and international events, that most of us, long ago, came to rely on the media and generally trust its ability to inform.

This section begins with an essay called, "Literacies and Media Literacy," examining the role of language and the functions of speaking, reading, and writing in communication. The concept of literacy is expanded in discussions about the variety of ways messages are sent and received in an era of media and computer communications. The next essay, "Violence in the Media," applies principles of media literacy to the topic of representational violence. It outlines several ways to think about this highly contested public issue. The final essay, "Technology and the Everyday," reviews both utopian and dystopian perspectives on new media technologies.

Literacies and Media Literacy

When most people hear the term "literacy," the first idea that comes to mind is written proficiency. A literate person is one who knows how to read and write. In the contemporary world, literacy is considered to be a prerequisite for success in school, careers, and everyday life. Students who do not learn to read and write properly are compromised in their ability to function fully in society. If a person cannot read, it is difficult to fill out a job application, get a driver's license, or access important news and information that may only be available in printed materials. Literacy also plays a crucial role in the maintenance of a healthy democracy. To participate in collective decisionmaking, citizens need to be able to access information, "read" the world around them, and respond in appropriate ways. Contrary to what many people think, literacy is a pertinent issue throughout the world and is not just a challenge faced in underdeveloped countries or inner cities. Literacy challenges exist in every neighborhood, every church group, every school, and every work environment. It's important to recognize that definitions of literacy vary. Also, literacy is relative to the nation or place in which it is measured. When the National Institute for Literacy speaks of literacy in the United States, it specifies "literacy" in English because it recognizes that non-English speakers may be perfectly functioning members of society. There is no single definition of literacy. In fact, the term "literacy" now extends far beyond mere spoken or written language. As Elizabeth Thoman and Tessa Jolls explain:

> Today, information about the world around us comes to us not only by words on a piece of paper but more and more through the powerful images and sounds of our multimedia culture. From the clock radio that wakes us up in the morning until we fall asleep watching the late night talk show, we are exposed to hundreds—even thousands—of images and ideas not only from television but also from websites, movies, talk radio, magazine covers, e-mail, video games, music, cell phone messages, billboards—and more. Media no longer just shape our culture … they *are* our culture.[2]

Although most people take for granted their abilities to decipher the meanings of photographs, television programs, movies, and other media, numerous complex audio/visual "languages" are used, each having specific rules and grammar. Thoman and Jolls assert,

"If our children are to be able to navigate their lives through this multimedia culture, they need to be fluent in 'reading' and 'writing' the language of images and sounds" just as they have learned to "read" and "write" the language of printed communications.[3]

In discussing media literacy, psychologist Howard Gardner explains that people possess not just one form of intelligence but what he terms "multiple intelligences." Gardner contends that "literacies, skills, and disciplines ought to be pursued as tools that allow us to enhance our understanding of important questions, topics, and themes."[4] Today's readers become literate by learning to read the words and symbols in today's world. Readers analyze, compare, evaluate, and interpret multiple representations from a variety of media formats, including spoken language, texts, photographs, moving pictures, and interactive media.

On a basic level, media literacy has evolved to help people understand the different ways that information is organized and presented in these audio/visual formats. Although everyone possesses a fundamental ability to understand a lecture, a photograph, or a television commercial—clearly we are in an era in which further education can help one grapple with the sensory overload that the more complicated forms of media utilize. Consider the ways these different forms of media deliver content.

Speaking is a linear, time-based form of expression. Words and sentences are uttered in a sequence that accumulates meaning as the speaker continues to talk. In classical Western philosophy, spoken language was said to operate through the principles of rhetoric and grammar. In ancient and medieval times, rhetoric (from the Greek word *rhêtôr* for orator or teacher) was the art or technique of persuasion through the use of oral language.[5] As such, rhetoric was said to flourish in open and democratic societies with rights of free speech, free assembly, and political enfranchisement for some portion of the population. In conjunction with rhetoric, grammar concerned itself with correct, accurate, pleasing, and effective language use through the study and criticism of literary models. Keeping track of rhetoric and grammar requires considerable concentration, since what is being said typically is not repeated. Listeners must follow the spoken sequence of ideas and construct the story or argument in their own minds. One advantage of conventional face-to-face spoken communication lies in its ability to convey added nuance and meaning through the intonation, facial expressions, pacing, and body language of the speaker (*ethos*). Also, listening makes demands on one's time. A person can read a book anywhere and anytime. But conversations or lectures are often fixed in time and space.

In today's digital world, much communication takes place by electronic means. People don't spend as much time as they once did sharing the same physical space for an exchange of ideas. In the 1800s, audiences would sit for prolonged periods to hear oratorical exchanges. Neil Postman writes that the famous presidential debate between Stephen A. Douglas and Abraham Lincoln on August 21, 1858, lasted seven hours, with each speaker debating and then responding for ninety minutes at a time.[6] Listeners can exert control over the speed of the communication only if in conversation with the speaker—or in a situation like a class or meeting, which would permit feedback during the discussion. Such instances afford participants in a dialogue to make observations, pose questions, or otherwise interact to change the course of the spoken narrative. Listeners must maintain attention to the speaker and make efforts to screen out extraneous sounds or goings on. The telephone facilitates this process in common usage by limiting communication to two conversants. Anyone who has ever joined a conference call will attest to the complexities of keeping track of the multiple voices, which have been stripped of their visual and spatial referents. People on conference calls need to tell others when they arrive or are leaving and continually need to remind each other who they are.

Written language also works in a linear sequence, but not with the same spontaneity of speaking. Because the narrative is printed on a page, readers have the ability to determine the pace of reading. At the same time, readers need to remain relatively immobile, concentrated on the text, and undistracted by extraneous design elements, typographic flourishes, or illustrations. In this sense, readers can exert a degree of control over the sequence of ideas they are given. Readers can pause, reread, skip ahead, or take breaks in their reading. But because the narrative is silently appearing on a page, readers have little opportunity to interact or respond to the writer or to gain the type of additional cues that speaking can express. Also unlike speaking, written texts can be shared with others or reengaged at other times. Indeed, the physicality of a printed text is one of its great advantages over spoken language. But this same physicality also tethers messages to the materiality of printed matter.

It took the introduction of the telegraph in the mid-1800s to mobilize the world of print by changing the speed by which information traveled. Prior to the telegraph, information could only move as fast as a ship or train could travel. With the telegraph, the huge time lapses that could fall between news and its reception at a distant location were eliminated. But the context from which news emerged was often lost in the process. As the speed of messages increasingly surpassed the ability of people to travel with them, telegraphed information began to take on a life of its own. Some historians of communication assert that this dematerialization of information ushered in a new age of deception and confusion—while at the same time allowing disembodied information to become commodified in new ways. Messages disconnected from any physical trace of their origin could be decontextualized and manipulated as never before.[7] A person on the West Coast could communicate via telegraph with a person on the East Coast, but not necessarily with any depth or background knowledge. As Postman writes, "The telegraph may have made the country into 'one neighborhood,' but it was a peculiar one, populated by strangers who knew nothing but the most superficial facts about each other."[8]

Sound recordings offer many of the benefits of written texts in the ways they allow readers/listeners options for reviewing or altering the pace of listening. Recorded information offers obvious benefits to the unsighted or to those without reading ability. Recorded texts also convey additional levels of meaning that come from inflection, intonation, multiple voices, and added elements like music or sound effects. But recordings require equipment that written texts do not. The benefit of sound equipment lies in its ability both to play and record information—and by extension makes the recordings available by duplication, amplification, or transmission to multiple listeners or remote audiences in much the same way printing functions for written texts. Recorded music is consumed by individuals, broadcast via radio or the Internet, compiled into collections, and in the digital age is shared among users, sampled, manipulated, and reused in new, creative contexts. Sound recordings do this in part by isolating a moment and then removing it from what falls outside the recording. This erases the surrounding information from which the recording was derived. Context disappears. At the same time, recordings exploit the viewer's trust in mechanically produced realism. Even though people know that sound recordings can distort reality or create alternative realities via analog or digital enhancement, people retain a belief in their verisimilitude even if it is a tentative belief. There is no other choice.

Photography delivers meaning in a nonsequential fashion, with the entire image available at once. With a photograph, a viewer has the ability to navigate the image, choosing where to look and what elements to scrutinize. For this reason, the meanings that photographs convey are less stable than sound recordings or written texts. What a photograph "says" to a viewer is in part dependent on how the viewer chooses to "read" the image. Photographic meaning also emerges from such elements of visual language as composition, shape, tone, color, point of view, image size, and cropping—all of which are operating simultaneously. These formal elements are but the beginning of the story, however. The content of the image, juxtaposition of subject matter, and the various interpretations that pictorial elements evoke work together to make photography an extremely dynamic medium. Complicating matters further are the accumulated meanings that come when several photographs are seen together on a page, or in sequence, or when captions or other texts accompany the images. The multiplicity of these factors explains why people often derive different meanings from photographs or at times can't explain why a photograph is saying what it is saying. Some communications' experts assert that the complexities of photographic language enable it to manipulate viewers, as happens in advertising, propaganda, and entertainment contexts.

Motion pictures combine the elements of movement, sequence, sound, and special effects with the delivery of photographic meaning. Individual shots are animated by action taking place within them, but further motion can be added with camera zooms, pans, and tracking techniques. These cinematic forms of movement geometrically extend the complexity of meaning beyond that of a still photograph. The sequencing of shots into a filmic montage adds another dimension. Dialogue, voiceovers, music, and sound effects contribute added layers of meaning. Conventional special effects and the plethora of contemporary digital enhancements, animation footage, and computer-generated imagery complicate interpretation still further. But like photographs, moving pictures construct a world of decontextualized fragments. Film and video clips exist without a connection to the world from which they were taken. They can be used for any purpose to say anything. As such, pieces of moving imagery have no certain history, veracity, or ethics. They are simply fragments of material.

Interactive media use computers or networks to enable the user to initiate communication or respond to it. It is often argued that interactive technologies are more potent than "passively" received media such as television and radio because users must actively participate in the experience of searching a text, playing a game, or writing an e-mail message. The nature of this interaction becomes exceedingly complex if audio/visual information and text are negotiated simultaneously with hand controls and steering mechanisms, and accompanied by the perception of rapid movement through space. The interactive character of computer networks has enabled the creation of online communities and new "spaces" of engagement for purposes ranging from game playing to academic research.

The two-directional information flow of interactive multimedia also has enabled industry and government to monitor online activity and collect information about users.

As even this brief review of media forms and technologies suggests, the various "languages" embedded in everyday communication, entertainment, and news media are considerably more complicated than many people perceive. Yet most of us take our fundamental "literacy" in these technologies for granted. Should we be concerned about media with such powerful abilities to manipulate information or influence opinion? Postman has argued that as we have evolved from a society based on the spoken or printed word to one based on photography, sound recordings, and moving pictures, we have gradually lost the ability to discern the veracity of what we are interpreting. Postman states, "Since intelligence is primarily defined as one's capacity to grasp the truth of things, it follows that what a culture means by intelligence is derived from the character of its important forms of communication."[9] Postman goes on to explain, "As a culture moves from orality to writing to printing to television, its ideas of truth move with it."[10]

With spoken and typographic media, many people feel more confident about their abilities to discern the truth of statements because they can examine messages in a controlled, word-by-word manner. Clear rules of syntax in oral and written communication have the effect of stabilizing meaning. But a photograph "lacks a syntax," according to Postman, "which deprived it of a capacity to argue with the world."[11] He claims that "As an 'objective' slice of space-time, the photograph testified that someone was there or something happened. Its testimony is powerful but offers no opinions—no 'should-have-beens' or 'might-have-beens.' Photography is preeminently a world of fact, not of dispute about facts or of conclusions to be drawn from them."[12] Making matters worse, photographs dislocate meaning in both time and space. Susan Sontag wrote about this ability of a photographic image to alter the interpretation of a scene, stating that the borders of a photograph "seem arbitrary. Anything can be separate, made discontinuous, from anything else: All that is necessary is to frame the subject differently."[13]

Cautionary voices like Postman's and Sontag's urge consideration of media and digital education in public policy debates, school curriculum discussions, and the programming of public service media. These advocates assert that in today's world a media/digital literate citizenry is a necessity for a healthy democracy. This type of literacy education begins with an analysis of how images on TV or on the Web are built in formal terms. It then moves to discussion of the producers, intentions, contexts, and economic issues behind visual material. These powerful concepts of electronic literacy can be used to enhance people's critical thinking skills about the mass media to help them look at television and interactive media in new ways, and to clarify the role that consumers play in the economics of media.

The Evolution of the Media Literacy Field

Television became a part of education in the United States during the decade following the Second World War, but critical viewing was the last thing from the minds of its early proponents. As the first wave of the baby boom hit the classroom in the 1950s, video was recognized as a means of increasing teacher productivity. By simply eliminating the need for duplicate presentations, video was credited with reductions in teaching labor of up to seventy percent.[14] Video was also recognized as a powerful tool for observation and evaluation.[15] Concurrent advances in computer and telecommunications industries prompted more elaborate speculation. While in residence at New York's Fordham University during the late 1960s, Marshall McLuhan attracted a quasi-religious following based on his vision of a global telecommunications network designed on biological (and therefore "natural") principles that would undermine all hierarchical structures. At the core of McLuhan's program lay a concept of media as "information without content" that defined international turmoil as the result of failed communication rather than ideological confrontation.[16]

This idealistic vision of new technology fit perfectly into 1960s educational reformism, while also complementing U.S. cultural policy. In a domestic atmosphere of desegregation, urban renewal, and other liberal initiatives, efforts were made to eliminate the biases inherent in traditional schooling. As a means of deemphasizing differences of race, gender, and class, theories of educational formalism were introduced into much instruction to stress the structure of learning over culturally specific content. Educators uncritically seized upon photographic media as tools for directly engaging student experience. They developed concepts of "visual literacy" to compete with what some viewed as oppressive print-oriented paradigms.[17] As one educational textbook of the era explained, many students "demonstrate a lack of proficiency and lack of interest in reading and writing. Can we really expect proficiency when interest is absent? To what purpose do we force students through traditional subjects in traditional curricula?"[18] Within this movement, many teachers adapted photography and video equipment to teach subjects ranging from social studies to English composition.

With the economic downturns of the 1980s, along with the ascendancy of the Reagan/Bush administration, came the sweeping indictments of government-supported liberal programs. Supply-side analysts blamed schools for the nation's inability to compete in world markets, while ironically arguing for reductions in federal education and cultural budgets. Because they often required expensive equipment, media programs were terminated in the name of cost reduction, as renewed emphasis was placed on a "back-to-basics" curriculum. This did not mean that television disappeared from the classroom, only that it's more complicated, hands-on applications were replaced by simple viewing.

The type of media that survived the reform movements of the early 1980s differed greatly from its utopian predecessors. Stripped of any remnant of formalist ideology, video was reduced to its utilitarian function as a labor-saving device. This redefinition of "television as teacher" paralleled distinct shifts in production and distribution. These were outgrowths of large-scale changes in the film and television industry brought about by the emergence of affordable consumer video cassette equipment. For the viewer, home recording and tape rental allowed hitherto unknown control over what was watched. The same was true in the classroom. For the instructional media industry, the costly process of copying 16mm films was quickly supplanted by inexpensive high speed video duplication. The entire concept of educational media products began to change, as films could be mass produced on a national scale (in effect "published") like books. Market expansion in this type of video was exponential. So profound was the technological change that 16mm film processing labs from coast to coast went out of business overnight.

Although the shape of education was changed forever, computers didn't become a serious part of K–12 schooling until the 1990s, with the broadbased distribution of personal computers in the home, the development of network technology, and the popular advocacy of computers in education by such public figures as Al Gore and Bill Gates. Like cable television, the Internet was touted as a means of bringing the outside world into the classroom, while connecting students to resources hitherto unimagined. In its early stages of implementation, school computerization was also regarded as a means of leveling the cultural differences among students—much as "visual literacy" had been promoted. These attitudes fit well within the progressive belief that digital media could deliver a world of great equity and freedom. From this perspective, public education should be seen as an extremely important means of redressing technological inequities and their inherent relationships with race, gender, geography, and social class. Not only can schools serve as places to provide access and instruction to digital media, but they can structure that experience of these media through progressive pedagogies that critically engage technologies and that foster equity and student agency. Is the current craze for computers in the classroom simply an extension of this historical faith in educational mechanization, or it something more?

The business interests that have the most to gain in this matter assert that fundamental structural changes and paradigm shifts are occurring that necessitate new technological approaches to schooling. This could be dismissed as simple self-interestedness were it not that high-tech corporations increasingly have a role in educational policy discussions. Meanwhile, parents exposed to an endless barrage of effusive media reports and advertising about the "information society" and the need for "digital literacy" are petrified at the idea of their kids missing out. So it's a double whammy. As parents pressure schools to adopt technology, schools are becoming institutional customers for educational products and venues for promotions targeted at students. It's an entrepreneurial dream come true. Fortunately, there are limits to ways that K–12 schools can tolerate change. Given their role as day care for underage youth, the fundamental structure of schools and the school day will not change significantly. Since primary and secondary schools are also regarded as a site for general academic or vocational education, the fundamental balance in curriculum among humanities, science, and math offerings will similarly resist significant change. This stability is further buttressed by the decentralized governance of schools at the level of the local school district and the high degree of political scrutiny that communities afford to educational issues. This raises the crucial issue of computer competency or what has been termed "digital literacy."

Contrary to the popular notion of young people as naturally computer savvy, a need exists to instill critical sensibilities toward digital media much like those offered by television- and film-oriented media literacy programs. Partly informed by critical pedagogy and cultural studies, the digital literacy movement (as opposed to its older market research counterpart) is an amalgam of reader-response theories and institutional analyses. While acknowledging the persuasive properties of images, practitioners of digital literacy emphasize ways that viewers use media in individualized ways. Moreover, because Web surfers and computer game players can recognize the artifice of representation, they need not always be fooled by it. The concept of literacy is central in this pedagogy, as explained by Cary Bazalgette: "Every medium can be thought of as a language. Every medium has its own way of organizing meaning, and we all learn to 'read' it, bringing our own understandings to it, and extending our own experience through it."[19]

The digital literacy movement holds political significance. Not only can it help viewers to "decode" complex sign systems, but it also can connect theory and practice—often by attempting to literally explain (or demonstrate) complex theories to young people. By doing this, it diplomatically reconciles opposing concepts of the viewing subject. The digital literacy movement argues that our abilities to mediate dominant readings and spectator positioning can be improved with study, and that these skills can be taught to children regardless of age or grade level. One can teach young people to use digital tools for their own ends by actively interpreting how the tools function and then choosing how to utilize them. Put another way, the movement proposes to begin identifying strategies for contextual reading, thereby suggesting changes to the "institutional structures" that condition spoken and interpretive norms.[20] This is done by encouraging viewers to look beyond specific texts by asking these critical questions: Who is communicating and why? How are the messages being produced? Who is receiving them and what sense do they make of it?

Violence in the Media

When concerns are voiced about excessive television viewing or video game playing, the worries generally relate to violent content. Media violence has motivated much of the debate over broadcast public policy for several decades and remains one of the most widely discussed yet little understood issues of our time. The ubiquity of violent imagery in everyday life makes it a topic about which everyone has an opinion. Yet the fractured and contradictory character of the public debate on media violence offers little insight. Instead, the discussion degenerates into arguments between those who fear and those who relish such material. Lost in these discussions are considerations of why violent representations are so common and how they satisfy certain audience desires. Also largely missing are discussions about the various stakeholders in the media violence debate: consumers, industry producers, child advocates, academic media "experts," outraged politicians, and journalists covering the issue. As an ensemble, these many voices create what might be termed "the media violence tower of babble."

In a now famous study conducted in the 1970s, a group of American researchers were convinced they'd come up with a perfect way to measure the effects of violent media.[21] The group had decided to study teenage boys who lived in residential facilities and boarding schools where television viewing could be completely controlled. For a period of six weeks, half of the boys were permitted to watch only violent programs and the other half nonviolent shows. Everyone expected the boys exposed to violence to become more aggressive and unruly, as similar studies of younger children had demonstrated. But the findings shocked everyone. As the weeks went by, the boys watching the nonviolent shows started fistfights and began vandalizing the schools. They disrupted classes and shouted expletives at teachers and each other, while the group viewing the violent shows remained peaceful and studious, even more so than usual.

The researchers were baffled. Maybe the violent shows had helped their viewers blow off steam with some kind of cathartic effect. But past studies of catharsis had shown that it varied dramatically from individual to individual and never lasted very long. Soon more experts began examining the findings, and eventually they came up with the answer. The group watching the nonviolent programs had become angry because they had been denied their favorite shows (they were especially upset about missing *Batman*). Viewing enjoyment or unhappiness, it turned out, played a much greater role in the boys' behavior than the amount of violence they saw. In fact, the media violence seemed to have no effect whatsoever.

The point of this anecdote is not to suggest that media violence is harmless. Research over the past decade has shown that violent media cause plenty of harm. But the dangers are not always the ones that seem most obvious. The commonsense assumptions that one draws from watching a four-year-old boy throw a karate kick like a

Teenage Mutant Ninja Turtle do not necessarily apply to a teenager, an eight-year-old, or even another preschooler. Like the boys in the residence homes, media affects people in highly individualized ways. By the same token, the social factors underlying aggression and crime are influenced by far more than violent media. After decades of pronouncements by headline-hungry politicians and pop psychologists that social problems might be fixed with better TV viewing habits and fewer video games, the consensus of academics, educators, and policy makers has begun to shift in recent years to a more holistic consideration of violent media and violent people.

Understanding the issue of media violence requires an approach that goes beyond simple arguments of condemnation or support. In questioning typical views of media violence, it is important to view the topic in a broader context—taking into account the social, economic, and political factors that encourage and thrive upon violent entertainment. Also worth consideration are the uses that violent stories play in education, art, and historical accounts of violent occurrences in human history resulting from war, genocide, and natural catastrophe. In addition, one should examine the distinctly American style of much media violence. Historically, the United States dominated global media production and was the source of most movies and television the world saw. The picture changed somewhat when multinational corporations began restructuring production and distribution in the 1980s and 1990s, but the influence of U.S. television and moviemaking has endured, even in the face of burgeoning media industries in other nations.

Beginning with a look at history, one should consider concerns about violent media that have accompanied the development of new communication media from the printing press to the Internet. Different stakeholders in the media violence debate—audiences, producers, and academics—often have viewed the topic in mutually exclusive, one-dimensional terms. One might ask why, in the face of so many efforts to curb the proliferation of violent material, media violence continues to escalate in new and more potent forms. Answering this question requires asking why media violence exists and how we can learn to deal with it.

The commonsense assumption that depictions of violence promote deviant behaviors predates the invention of film and television. Victorian-era street theater and penny novels were thought to encourage misbehavior among the working poor, especially young men in urban areas.[22] Indeed, some accounts of the media violence debate date to Aristotle, as long ago as 400 B.C. For this reason, any serious examination of media violence needs to begin by examining historical continuities in the public concern over violent expression, while also noting the unique ways that different media convey violence. Questions need to be asked about why, after decades of public debate, policy analysis, and academic scrutiny, the discourse on media violence remains riven with inconsistency. While certain groups of researchers (primarily in the social sciences) continue to assert that violence in media is bad, firm conclusions about why it is bad have failed to materialize. In part, this results from difficulties in consistently defining "media violence."

What Is Media Violence?

The media violence question has resisted resolution in part because the topic is so hard to define. At first, most people have no trouble calling to mind a violent image from a cop show, horror movie, or video game. But is media violence simply a matter of depicting physical harm? Does it need to be aggressive or intentional? What about accidents or natural disasters? Does psychological torment count? What about verbal or implied violence? Are there degrees of violence? Is justified violence better for viewers than the gratuitous variety? What about humorous violence? Sports? How about violent documentaries? Or the nightly news?

Part of the problem is that violent representations are so deeply ingrained in our culture. For centuries, violence has been an important element of storytelling, and violent themes appear in the classical mythology of many nations, masterpieces of literature and art, folk lore and fairy tales, opera, and theater. Religious texts—the Bible and the Koran—use episodes of violence to dramatize moral lessons and to teach people to care for each other. Fairy tales warn children about the violent consequences of not behaving as instructed by adults. Great paintings and public monuments record human history with depictions of violence. And what about violence today? Eliminating violence from home entertainment has become a lot more feasible now that TVs are built with V-chips. But what would be the result of eliminating violence? Getting rid of offerings like *Fear Factor* and *28 Weeks Later* (2007) on the basis of violence alone would also rule out important films like *Saving Private Ryan* (1998), *Schindler's List* (1993), and *Hotel Rwanda* (2004)—not to mention children's classics from *The Lion King* (1994) to *Bridge to Terabithia* (2007).

The ubiquity of violent representations has made them a part of everyday life, and their volume keeps growing. Pick up any newspaper or turn on the TV and you will find either violent imagery or a story about violent media. Like the war on poverty, the war on drugs, and the war on terrorism, campaigns to stem the tide of media violence have failed. The most systematic quantitative studies of media violence are those conducted about television, where the frequency of violent incidents can be assessed relative to total programming. Some of the more alarmist voices in the media violence field have claimed a young person will witness two hundred thousand simulated violent acts and sixteen thousand dramatized murders by the age of eighteen.[23]

Researchers studying media violence have attempted to arrive at scientific definitions in efforts to measure media violence. In the 1960s and 1970s, this often meant something as simple as counting the number of times a character threw a punch or shot a gun, with incidents on *Colombo, Star Trek,* and *Get Smart* all given the same weight. No distinctions were drawn between realism, fantasy, or comedy until the 1980s, when some researchers began considering the plausibility or effects of violent incidents, as well as psychological aggression. Efforts to define media violence reached a watershed moment in the mid-1990s, when a consortium of research universities conducted the National Television Violence Study (NTVS), analyzing more than ten thousand hours of broadcast material. Studying twenty-three channels, the NTVS found eighteen thousand violent acts for each week of programs it analyzed—or six-and-a-half incidents per channel per hour. The study determined that the average adult watched four hours of television each day.[24] Children watched three hours a day.[25] These patterns persist. Violence is seen on TV by people of all ages. In addition to the violence seen regularly in television dramas, sports, and Saturday morning cartoons, news coverage of war, terrorism, and crime has increased the sense of immediacy and realism in televisual violence. This has been amplified by the rise of reality-based programs and the generalized message that the world is becoming a more dangerous place.

The NTVS study was the first of its size to argue the importance of context in considering violent material, making the startling statement that "not all depictions of violence are harmful."[26] It makes a difference, the NTVS stated, whether the violence is presented graphically on-screen or simply implied. It matters what type of character commits the violence, why, and with what kind of consequence. Is the violence committed by a hero or "good guy"? Is the action justified or rewarded? Does the violence cause pain and suffering? Or perhaps it seems to have no effect at all, as in many cartoons and comedy programs. Do we sympathize with the victim? Or not? Finally, who is the audience for the violence? The NTVS argued forcefully that not all people react to violence in the same way. The point is that not all media violence is created equal. But rarely are these many distinctions and nuances mentioned in public debates over these issues.

The potency of violent depictions in movies is continually enhanced by computer-generated special effects. This not only makes for more spectacular pyrotechnics, it also has blurred the line between reality and fantasy as never before. The incidence of gore may not have increased over that brought to movies by the "new violence" directors of the 1990s, such as Abel Ferrara, Oliver Stone, and Quentin Tarantino, but the formal means by which violence could be visualized and thus imagined grew with advances in technology. Science fiction films like *X-Men: The Last Stand* (2006) and *They Came From Upstairs* (2008) introduce new kinds of blasters, phasers, and aliens as horror films like *Ghost Rider* (2007) and *Near Dark* (2008) suggest vampires and other killers can materialize just about anytime from thin air. A spate of war films like *Troy* (2004), *Flyboys* (2006), and *300* (2007) use digital technology to bring thousands of combatants to the screen, as have fantasy movies like the *Lord of the Rings* trilogy (2000–2004). Popular imports like *Ichi the Killer* (2002), *The Grudge 2* (2006), and *Amu* (2007) have vividly portrayed mass murder and suicide—often focusing on teenage victims—as computer effects have allowed martial arts films like *House of Flying Daggers* (2005), *Two Kings* (2007), and *Five Venoms* (2008) to launch physical combat into supernatural dimensions. Some analysts assert that the aesthetics of media violence simply satisfies existing audience desires for violent fare. In the 1960s, anthropologist Karl Lorenz argued that primitive instincts in people make them seek out stimulating experiences.[27] George Gerbner has concluded in what he terms "cultivation theory" that viewers become acclimated to ever more potent forms of violent representation that raise their thresholds for such material and heighten the level of intensity of programs they seek.[28] Dolf Zillman has made similar assertions in a variety of his articles and research papers. It's worth noting in this context that some researchers have argued media violence is less appealing to audiences than TV formats like comedy or game shows.

Media Violence Then and Now

Violence has always figured prominently in storytelling. Violent imagery has been around since hunters began scratching accounts of their exploits on the walls of caves. Whether or not one believes that violent behavior is an innate part of human nature, violence has always played a major role in storytelling. Artifacts of Egyptian, Sumerian, Minoan, and Babylonian peoples all depict violent events, as do classical works of the ancient Greeks written three thousand years ago. All rely on violence to propel their narratives. Homer's *Iliad* (c. 760) relentlessly recounts military conflict, assassination, mass execution, sexual assault, and natural disaster. The same holds true for the *Odyssey* (c. 680), Hesiod's *Theogony* (c. 700), Aeschylus' *Oresteia* (c. 458), Sophocles' *Oedipus the King* (c. 428), and Thucydides' *History of the Peloponnesian War* (c. 424–440). The books of the Old Testament, written during the same period, are filled with accounts of genocide, war, human sacrifice, and, of course, various plagues. And as actor/director Mel Gibson so eloquently reminded moviegoers with his hugely successful film, *The Passion* (2004), the biggest story of the New Testament culminates in rioting, ritual torture, and public execution. Perhaps more to the point, these grisly stories have been repeated for centuries to children and adults alike as important works of history and religion.

The pattern continues in the centuries to follow, suggesting that violence is deeply embedded in the type of stories from Western civilization. Literary works of the Middle Ages like Dante's *Inferno* (1302) and Chaucer's *Canterbury Tales* (1386–1400) were riddled with detailed descriptions of violent assault and death. The best-known plays of William Shakespeare, including *Hamlet* (1607), *Julius Caesar* (1600), *Macbeth* (1606), *Othello* (1605), and *Romeo and Juliet* (1595) relied heavily on patricide, fratricide, suicide, and plain old murder to drive their plots. These works by Shakespeare were, in their day, the cultural equivalent to *Desperate Housewives* and *CSI*. Everybody saw them, from the illiterate "groundlings" who sat on the floor of the public theater to university-educated elites or those who might attend special performances of the plays at Queen Elizabeth's court.

The printing press enabled dissemination of these and other works beyond the stage. Guttenberg's invention of moveable type in 1452 and the subsequent development of vellum paper meant that by the mid-1500s more than one thousand print shops were operating in Europe. As printing improved over the next century, "true crime" books began recounting criminal acts and the brutal punishments that awaited those apprehended for them. The books satisfied a hunger for gore and provided warnings for potential offenders. It's probably worth mentioning that during this era public executions took place regularly in most European countries, attracting huge audiences for violent displays of state authority. By the middle of the eighteenth century, the modern novel was born with the publication of Samuel Richardson's *Pamela* (1741), and with it came the first public outcries over the effects of media. [29] Richardson's story of a virtuous servant girl preyed upon by an unscrupulous seducer was excoriated in tracts circulated throughout

London, condemning it for "lewdness" and for assaulting "principles of virtue."[30]

The contemporary era of American media violence debates began in the 1960s. After decades of self-regulation, the media industries in the United States began reintroducing violence and sex that had been forbidden in film and TV by the Production Code, which was in effect from 1930 to 1958. The Production Code had been written and enforced by the major movie studios to head off any regulation efforts by the government. With the decline of the Hollywood studio system following World War II, the structural underpinning of industry restraint loosened. At the same time, the mood of social activism in the United States emboldened filmmakers to think more independently. In particular, the Vietnam War fostered a national conversation about the nature of aggression and conflict. The result was more violence on the screen. Movies either reveled in gore or used it to awaken audiences to consequences of aggression in films ranging from *Psycho* (1960) and *The Misfits* (1961) to *Bonnie and Clyde* (1967) and *Night of the Living Dead* (1968). Director Sam Peckinpah asserted that he lengthened the gunfight scenes in his western *The Wild Bunch* (1968) to impress audiences with the true horror of combat. But what really worried people was sex. Films like *Who's Afraid of Virginia Woolf?* (1966) and *Blow Up* (1966) pushed the envelope of what could be said and shown with explicit language and graphic footage. In 1968, newly installed president of the Motion Picture Association of America Jack Valenti announced implementation of the voluntary movie rating system that would evolve into G, PG, PG-13, R, and NC-17, which is still used today.

The media again came under public scrutiny in the culture wars of the 1980s. Entertainment and the arts, along with schools, were blamed with weakening intellectual and moral fiber in the United States and other nations. But Americans led the way in calling for a return to traditional values and education. During the Reagan administration, the office of the attorney general was charged with policing culture though the infamous Meese Commission on Pornography, which convened from 1985 to 1986. Although the Meese Commission succeeded in drawing public attention to pornography, it did little to change the sex industry and had no legislative impact whatsoever.

Changes did occur in the music industry, which was transformed in the 1980s by two phenomena: MTV and hip-hop. Vividly brought to life in music videos, explicit song lyrics provided the impetus for the formation of the Parent's Music Resource Council (PMRC), organized in 1985 by Tipper Gore (spouse of former vice president Al Gore) and Susan Baker (wife of former Reagan White House Chief of Staff James Baker). The group came into being, as the story goes, when the Gore family (including twelve-year-old Karinna) heard the word "masturbation" while listening to Prince's *Purple Rain* album. Gore quickly assembled sixteen other "Washington wives" and drew up a list of the "Filthy Fifteen" for presentation to Congress. Asserting that Prince's "Darling Nikki" and Madonna's "Dress You Up" were responsible for rising rape and suicide rates among those between ages sixteen and twenty-four, the PMRC garnered so much legislative support so quickly that the recording industry voluntarily developed its now well-known "Parental Advisory" labels before any laws were ever written. The television industry similarly initiated a voluntary program-labeling system in anticipation of the 1990 Television Violence Act requiring it to do so. Responding to criticism that the television labeling system was ineffective, letter coding was added in 1997 to indicate contents with "coarse language, sex, violence, and sexual dialogue."[31]

By the late 1990s, a broad-based consensus had solidified around the commonsense notion that violence in the media must produce violence at home and in the streets. This consensus was supported primarily by a number of widely publicized studies conducted within a subdiscipline of psychological research. Arguably the most frequently cited summary document is the 1999 *American Academy of Pediatrics and the American Academy of Child and Adolescent Psychiatry's Joint Statement on the Impact of Entertainment Violence on Children.*[32] The report asserts that more than one thousand studies "point overwhelmingly to a causal connection between media violence and aggressive behavior in some children."[33] A meta-analysis, the joint statement draws upon prior studies rather than research conducted by either professional organization. A similar statement issued in 1993 from the American Psychological Association said that "there is no doubt that higher levels of viewing violence are correlated with increased acceptance of aggressive attitudes and increased aggressive behavior."[34] It's important to note that the APA did not state that media *cause* aggression, only that a correlation was identified. In other words, aggressive individuals may consume violent media without it being the reason for the aggression. Due to the ambiguity in these findings, U.S. Surgeon General David Sachter would not list exposure to violent media as a cause of behavioral violence among young people, observing that it is "extremely difficult to distinguish between the relatively small long-term effects of exposure to media violence and those of other influences."[35]

Continued arguments that television carried too much sex and violence led to the provision requiring television sets made after 2000 to contain the V-chip, an electronic component allowing the selective blocking of programs with certain ratings. Ironically, as the number of TVs equipped with the protective technology has grown, most parents have no idea how the V-chip works or know that their TV set even contains one. In a survey by the Kaiser Family Foundation, only fifteen percent of parents reported using the V-chip. Many respondents (thirty-nine percent) didn't realize that their new TV sets were equipped with a V-chip, while others (twenty percent) knew they had a V-chip, but didn't use it. More to the point, even if parents knew how to use it, for the V-chip to be effective in blocking programming, TV networks would need to consistently identify program content with labels shown at the beginning of programs (such as "V" for violence, "L" for harsh language, "S" for sexual material, and "D" for sexual dialogue). Such labels do not appear on all shows. The story is the same for Internet use. While most parents have heard about the widely publicized dangers of Internet porn and sexual predators lurking in chat rooms, most parents either do not have or do not know if they have software on their computers that monitors where children go online or with whom they interact.[36] Finally, in a survey sure to drive some parents crazy, it was discovered that fifty percent of young people use the Internet while also watching television.[37]

In the years since 2000—and especially since 9/11—the media violence debate momentarily lost the frenzy of concern seen in the 1990s. A growing number of researchers have recanted dire predictions of the negative effects of violent movies and computer games, as scholars from the humanities and social sciences have added more nuance and complexity to the discussion. In 2001, a group of media scholars asked the American Academy of Pediatrics and the American Academy of Child and Adolescent Psychiatry to reconsider their joint policy statement issued that year on media violence because of its "many misstatements about social science research on media effects." The group of scholars—that included such notable intellectuals as Jib Fowles, Henry Giroux, Vivian Sobchack, and Pulitzer Prize laureate Richard Rhodes, cited the statement's factual inaccuracies and its "overall distortions and failure to acknowledge many serious questions about the interpretation of media violence studies."[38] Subsequently, a research subculture began developing around the examination of positive aspects of media and game culture. A notable example of this scholarship is represented in James Gee's *What Video Games Have to Teach Us About Literacy and Learning.* [39] In this work, Gee takes a cautious look at the neurological processing skills that game technologies help develop, without leaping to the conclusions of more hyperbolic writers in this area like Steven Johnson, author of *Everything Bad Is Good for You.* [40]

The Aesthetics of Violence

People take pleasure in media violence because it is no longer real. The aesthetics of pictures makes them dazzling or even beautiful. Contemporary violent films use an elaborate array of devices that viewers have come to accept as real. Multicamera cinematography records action from many angles and perspectives, quick-paced montage editing heightens perceptions of fast movement and excitement, slow motion segments draw attention into the scene and heighten the illusion of verisimilitude, and audio effects in the Foley studio and dramatic music stir excitement further. All of this contributes to what Stephen Prince termed a "stylistic rendition of violence." Writing of Sam Peckinpah's stylistic renderings, Prince describes a three-part process of montage construction: "The relatively simple, slow-motion insert crosscut into the body of a normal-tempo sequence; the synthetic superimposition of multiple lines of action with radical time-space distortions in a montage set-piece; and montages approaching Eisenstein's notion of intellectual editing, wherein the viewer is moved to cognitively grasp psychological or social truths."[41]

Because people want to see violent images, works using violence become commodities. Whether one blames supply or demand, the market for media violence remains intact, vibrant, and growing. People like media violence, often for the wrong reasons. It gets attention quickly and spices up movies, TV shows, and games. It lives in the culture of masculinity, strength, and national power. Images of suffering can turn into objects separated from the thing itself. People look at the images without seeing the actual pain. This can have a number of effects. Roland Barthes believed that shocking images of human suffering send us the message that horror has already happened and is over. The pictures offer evidence of something the viewer will not experience. Barthes writes, "Such images do not compel us to action, but to acceptance. The action has already been taken, and we are not implicated."[42] Put another way, the images tell us that we are safe and that the violence in the picture has been done to someone else—often in a faraway land.

Media violence is made attractive by artists and technicians. Most of what we see isn't real. The audiences won't tell you that because they don't fully want to admit that they know what they are viewing is a contrivance—a make-believe violent explosion, catastrophe, or fight—that serves as a stand-in for the real thing that they cannot bear or do not know. As photographer Alfredo Jarr wrote, the camera never really records the full experience of what one sees.[43] It records an abstraction of the event. In one of society's great ironies, pictures of violence sometimes become regarded as great art. They imbue transcendental meaning, even beauty, and if such images are in short supply they accrue great monetary value to those willing to pay. When violent images are plentiful, another irony transpires as they lose meaning in their abundance. Any single story of suffering becomes lost in an ocean of represented suffering. Personal tragedies multiply into a statistical report of losses. Or they are intentionally minimized by the bureaucratic language of casualties or "collateral damage."

Narratives of Violence

Media violence enlivens stories and is a part of stories that need telling. Excitement comes from the anticipation and experience of vicarious violence. It's like salt on food. Everybody likes it even though it's not good for you. The entertainment industry may capitalize on the human appetite for violence, but it doesn't create the hunger. For this reason, violence has become an ingredient of fairy tales and fiction writing, most top-grossing movies, the majority of what we see on TV, and what people want in video games. And much of the violence in entertainment that breaks box office records isn't really that violent after all. It's noise and light and special effects that in a funny way make people comfortable because the representations of violence seem so familiar. Because what audiences really want is the comfort of a familiar story. CBS mega-executive Leslie Moonves said that audiences don't like dark outcomes. "They like story. They do not respond to nervous breakdowns and unhappy episodes that lead nowhere. They like their characters to be part of the action. They like strength, not weakness."[44] They like the excitement in their stories—and media violence provides that excitement.

Some media producers have attempted to turn this taste for violence back upon itself by upsetting the familiar ways violence was portrayed. Avant-garde artists had long theorized that audiences would be shaken out of complacency by radically "new" ways of seeing things. Could a movie shock an audience that much? In the 1960s director Sam Peckinpah made the claim that his movie *The Wild Bunch* (1969) was intended as a statement of protest against the war in Vietnam. In the movie, a group of aging U.S. outlaws tries to rob a bank in Texas and then escaped to Mexico. There they try to steal a shipment of guns from a Mexican general. In the process, lots of gunfighting takes place, and many, many people get killed. The violence is extremely graphic, so graphic that people viewing the film frequently remarked that it had gone too far in making the bloodshed too "real." Stephen Prince has written extensively about Peckinpah's moviemaking and the many innovations that Peckinpah brought to the craft of putting a film together. He has made the important point that what Peckinpah achieved was to make viewers believe that what they were seeing was real using a sophisticated combination of techniques and filmmaking tricks. But most importantly, Prince believed that Peckinpah meant what he said about trying to make people feel sympathy for the victims and combatants of war. Peckinpah said that "we watch our wars and see men die, really die, every day on television, but it doesn't seem real. We don't believe those are real people dying on the screen. We've been anesthetized by the media. What I do is show people what it's really like…. To negate violence it must be shown for what it really is, a horrifying, brutalizing, destructive, ingrained part of humanity."[45]

Peckinpah learned some of what he knew about portraying violence from the films of Akira Kurosawa. In Kurosawa's movies many cameras were used to catch the action from different angles and the footage was cut in short segments to dramatize the action. To add further intensity, Kurosawa would alternate slow-motion and normal-speed footage to jar viewers into paying attention. Kurosawa also would use long telephoto lenses to focus attention on important elements in scenes. With the support of Warner Brothers Studio, Peckinpah was able to take these techniques and make a movie on a scale that Kurosawa could not. Peckinpah brought it all together in the spectacular gunfight massacres in *The Wild Bunch*, and audiences went wild over the movie. Many later films were styled on the model Peckinpah created.

Computer games add fresh dimensions to the aesthetics of media violence. They have become the leading source of violent entertainment—market penetration in 2005 for games, for the first time, surpassed fifty percent of the U.S. population.[46] People around the world now spend twice as much each year on computer games ($31 billion) as they do on movies ($14 billion).[47] The Entertainment Software Association asserts that adult game players (thirty-nine percent of whom are women) spend seven-and-a-half hours per week engaged in the activity and that eighty-four percent of people playing computer games are over the age of eighteen.[48] Some in the media violence community believe that the interactive character of computer games makes them a more influential "teacher" of aggressive behavior than movies or television, although such assertions have yet to be proven conclusively by scientific research. Regardless of its effects, computer gaming has become an enormous business—with the budgets of game development and promotion now surpassing that of many feature films. This is hardly surprising in light of the fact that popular games like *Grand Theft Auto: San Andreas* (2004) and *Halo 2* (2004) both sold more than 2.4 million copies (retailing at $49.95) on their first day of release, putting them on an economic par with the most successful Hollywood movies. With twelve million units sold, the number one game of 2007 was *Legend of Zelda: The Ocarina of Time,* which placed participants in an environment where they constantly battled with swords and slingshots.[49]

The New Economics of Entertainment

Without a doubt, the single most important factor in the ongoing presence of media violence is the dramatic change that has occurred in recent decades in the economic structure of the entertainment industry. The continuing consolidation of movie, television, and publishing companies and their acquisition by large, multinational corporations has resulted in operating philosophies and business procedures unlike those of the movie studios, television networks, and publishing houses that people once knew. Gone are the days of Hollywood moguls with stables of legendary movie stars making pictures on the basis of personal taste and creative instinct. Television is no longer the province of network executives who might champion situation comedies, long-form dramatic series, or Pulitzer Prize–winning news departments. And publishing is now completely a numbers game, with boutique presses and idiosyncratic novels giving way to million-copy press runs and blockbuster titles designed for maximum exposure on television talk shows and Barnes and Noble bookshelves.

These media industries have been changed by an accelerating pattern of corporate mergers and acquisitions that has been occurring during the past twenty-five years, and which gained tremendous momentum in the past decade. Actually, the process began well before that—as movie studios, broadcast networks, and publishers began merging and buying one another primarily in the years following World War II. But in more recent decades, huge multimedia empires have swallowed these discrete media companies, or gigantic corporations have acquired them with little intrinsic interest in movies or television or news, but with a big interest—indeed an all-consuming mandate—in satisfying the demands of corporate investors for continuing profits. This has meant that money—not ethics, or taste, or politics—has become the driving force in entertainment and journalism. And that is one of the biggest reasons why the flow of media violence has become nearly unstoppable.

Six multinational corporations now control the major U.S. media: Rupert Murdoch's News Corporation (FOX, HarperCollins,

New York Post, Weekly Standard, TV Guide, DirecTV, and thirty-five TV stations); General Electric (NBC, CNBC, MSNBC, Telemundo, Bravo, Universal Pictures, and twenty-eight TV stations); Time Warner (AOL, CNN, Warner Bros., *Time,* and its 130-plus magazines); Disney (ABC, Disney Channel, ESPN, ten TV stations, and seventy-two radio stations); Viacom (CBS, MTV, Nickelodeon, Paramount Pictures, Simon & Schuster, and 183 U.S. radio stations); and Bertelsmann (Random House and its more than 120 imprints worldwide, and Gruner + Jahr and its more than 110 magazines in ten countries).[50]

Is this consolidation of media ownership good or bad? Some people argue that bigger is better because it results in more economic muscle and greater economies of scale. These factors, it is argued, combine to reduce business operating expenses and as a consequence yield higher returns for corporate investors and lower prices for consumers—what business people like to call a "win-win" situation. Many of these efficiencies derive from the globalization of corporations, which allows them to sell their products around the world, decentralize the manufacture of goods, utilize labor pools in nations where people work for little money, and negotiate favorable trade relationships. The downside of all of this is that corporate consolidation, for all of its apparent benefits, often harms the very people and nations its advocates claim to be helping. This is because the corporate profits, bargain-priced goods, and great trade arrangements tend to benefit most the wealthy and powerful people who run the corporations and make the deals. As a consequence, the rich of the world get richer and the poor get poorer. What effect does this new economic environment have on media violence? To answer that question one needs to examine the different ways movies, television, publishing, and, more recently, computer games and digital media, have responded to the new money game.

Technologies and the Everyday

Any discussion of everyday life needs to contain a consideration of "digital culture" and the technological values it promotes. Pick up any newspaper or magazine, or turn on a television, and you will see endless advertisements and news items suggesting that the latest digital phone, palm computer, minidisk player, or chip-implanted credit card will yield increased productivity, enlivened leisure time, and enhanced communication—not to mention social harmony, economic stability, and democracy.[51] Unlike prior utopias brought about by philosophical reflection, social amelioration, or proletarian revolt, this version of the future emerges as a product of a different sort. With the purchase of the appropriate products and services, a perfected existence will come from a multinational corporation.

This vision isn't so new, really. Throughout history, business interests have cloaked their agendas in a rhetoric of social betterment. General Electric's familiar "better living through technology" mantra of the 1950s was really just another way of focusing consumer attention on the added convenience of electric frying pans, blenders, and dishwashers—and away from the specters of industrial pollution, nuclear annihilation, and the forces of a predatory market capitalism. Indeed the purpose of advertising has always been to sell the idealized images that lie behind commodities, rather than merely the products themselves. In our hypersaturated media environment, the relationship of representations to their referents becomes reversed. Commercial images do not represent products as much as products represent images.[52]

So what is new about the utopia offered by cyberculture, if anything? In part, the answer lies in the extent that this utopia endlessly is hyped and promoted. But in another sense, digital media present novel and not entirely understood modes of experience that extend subjectivity, social relations, and political power into increasingly ephemeral and elusive dimensions. As people spend more and more time with their telephones, televisions, and computers, the physicality of experience diminishes. This has specific consequences for the world of commerce, where the production and sale of goods and services increasingly moves from the material to the immaterial. Concepts and images—termed "intellectual capital"—now dominate a marketplace previously devoted to the exchange of objects. In this environment, new currencies emerge relating to speed, access, and privacy. How fast a connection can one afford? How much hardware is needed? Where, when, and at what price can one access information? At how many points are one's movements and choices observed, recorded, analyzed, and sold?

Current controversies over the role of digital media in contemporary life have their roots in unresolved contradictions in the history of technology itself. As an area of study, technology largely was ignored through much of Western history. In the aristocratic culture of ancient Greece, the most revered forms of thinking addressed social, political, and theoretical concerns rather than what were considered the everyday banalities of technology.[53] Not unlike contemporary attitudes toward "technical schools" and "technicians," the idea of technology carried a crudely instrumental connotation. The conceptualization of "technology" in today's inclusive and comprehensive understanding of the term did not gain popular currency until after World War I. As the Western enlightenment was unfolding in the 1700s, technical ideas were considered endeavors in what were termed the "mechanical arts" (material, practical, industrial), as opposed to the "fine arts" (ideal, creative, intellectual). As Leo Marx writes, "The habit of separating the practical and the fine arts served to ratify a set of overlapping invidious distinctions between things and ideas, the physical and the mental, the mundane and the ideal female and male, making and thinking, the work of enslaved and free men."[54] This is not to suggest a negative view of technology—simply a resolutely practical one.

With the development of the biological and social sciences in the eighteenth and nineteenth centuries, technology came to be viewed as a natural manifestation of the human will to grow and prosper. This idea of technology as an organic and unremittingly positive "extension of man" provided the basis for what has been termed "technological instrumentalism." Within this commonsense framework, technology is viewed as a neutral tool that serves as an agent of social progress. Technological instrumentalism flourished in the nineteenth century with the development of such devices as the steam engine, locomotive, water mill, cotton gin, power loom, telegraph, and numerous other inventions that enhanced human capacity and industrial productivity. Ruminating over these innovations in his famous "Sign of the Times" essay of 1829, Thomas Carlisle termed the coming era the "Age of Machinery."[55] But the technological revolution had other consequences as well. With the broad-based mechanization of the workplace, the character of labor began to change, as goods once made by hand were produced on the assembly line. Over time, the culture of the everyday became controlled. As shoemakers, blacksmiths, and similar craftspeople were displaced by workers who operated machinery and punched a time clock, trades of many types became drained of their "artistic" elements. Attitudes toward work and leisure began to shift as a result. To a large extent, creative activity ceased to be a part of one's workplace activity, but instead was redefined as something experienced off the clock.

Paralleling this mechanization of everyday experience of work was the development of large-scale integrated "technological systems" to make such mechanization possible. Between 1870 and 1920 in the United States, enormous growth occurred in the development of electric power and light companies, telegraph and telephone systems, the chemical industry, transportation systems, and large-scale manufacturing. The mass production and distribution of a commodity like an automobile called into existence a complex constellation of variously skilled workers, suppliers, subcontractors, managers, supervisors, clerks, transporters, dealers, and service people. Railroad systems developed networks of tracks, equipment, conductors, communication networks, and ticket agents. Power grids were called into being as highways and housing developments sprang up across the nation.

Complimenting this thoroughly modern evolution in material goods were similarly scientific methods of everyday management. In this era the doctrines of Taylorsim and Fordism emerged to enhance worker efficiency and workplace productivity, as employees came to be seen more as components of the larger technological system than as individuals. As labor became fragmented and systemized, new regimes of rationality, efficiency, and order emerged in the edifice of impersonal bureaucracies and hierarchical administrative structures. In an atmosphere of economic growth driven by the imperatives of the modern corporation, the ethos of the day was continual acceleration and accumulation. Over time, technology became invested with "a host of metaphysical properties and potencies, thus making it seem a determinate entity, a disembodied, autonomous, causal agent of social change—of history."[56] The legacy of these early technological systems and their ideological underpinnings of the everyday are still with us today, manifest in the burgeoning bioscience and information technology sectors that the popular media tell us are fueling the nation's economic recovery.

It is important to acknowledge the range of counterarguments that have arisen to the systemization of everyday experience—and especially during the post–World War II years—to question, contradict, and negate the unproblematized premises of such utopian visions of technological progress. Historian Andrew Feenberg has used the term "technological substantivism" to describe various strains of opposition to the overriding discourse of technological instrumentalism.[57] Substantive analyses do not see technology as neutral, but instead view it as the embodiment of social values. An early skeptic of instrumentalism, Martin Heidegger wrote that technology invariably creates relationships of control from which people struggle in vain to free themselves. As a substance existing throughout human history, the hidden secret of technology as a controlling force became manifest in the modern era. "It is impossible," Heidegger wrote, "for man to imagine a position outside of technology."[58]

Jacques Ellul, among other substantive critics, further elaborated on the distinct relationship of technology to daily life. To Ellul, "technology has become autonomous" in its ability to structure human actions and relationships. Ellul was responding specifically to the way technological systems of the early twentieth century became transformed into "technocracies"—or technological bureaucracies—in which technology evolves into a branch of politics.[59] Within the autonomous logic of the technocracy, the original scientific impetus to develop systems for the Enlightenment goal of a better and more egalitarian society became subverted by the solipsistic imperatives of technology itself. Ellul's technocracies are self-replicating systems in which every action is rationalized as a contribution to technological improvement and expansion. As such, they constitute one of the primary means by which the Weberian iron cage of bureaucracy becomes actualized.

These generalized notions of technological substantivism assumed a degree of heightened potency and specificity in the years following World War II. With Hiroshima, the nuclear arms race, and the U.S. involvement in the Vietnam War, public anxieties began to erode the unquestioned role of technology as an instrument of social good. As a myriad of technologically based domestic products, like television, were introduced into the home, other voices were beginning to point out the environmental devastation created by unchecked industrial expansion. By the end of the 1960s, the student movements of the New Left had given technocracy a name—the "military-industrial complex"—and were blaming it for a plethora of social ills ranging from ecological devastation to the corporate transformation of the university into the "multiversity." Activists sought a structural reorganization of technocracy to better serve the interests of democracy. Such sentiments deepened in the 1980s with the 1984 leakage of poisonous gas from a Union Carbide Plant in Bhopal, India; the 1986 explosion of the Chernobyl Nuclear Power Plant in Russia; the 1989 Exxon Valdez oil spill off the shores of southeast Alaska; growing recognition of the phenomena of acid rain, ozone depletion, and global warming; and the social devastation of rust-belt communities brought on by the collapse of heavy industry.

Slowly the topic of technology in everyday life began to emerge as an issue of intellectual concern in a variety of disciplines. In addition to critiques from the antiwar and environmental movements, important analyses of technology emerged from Marxist, feminist, and poststructuralist circles. The Marxist arguments addressed the overarching linkage of technology to markets. As discussed by Andrew Ross, early on, technology was "dealt a hand in the power structure of capitalism (which is increasingly dependent on science-based industry), while its efficiency logic came to prevail over scientific management of everyday life."[60] The systematic effects of such social engineering have been widespread, from the reorganization of labor to the industrialization of culture and entertainment. This materialist critique differs from the substantive view of technology as a menace in its own right. Although lending itself easily to market exploitation, technology in this view was more a means than an end. As Ross concludes, "Capitalist reason, not technical reason, is still the order of the day."[61]

Feminist views of everyday technologies grew, at first, from critiques of science as a patriarchal system practiced by men and for men. Writers like Sandra Harding considered technology in epistemological terms, asking: Whose interests are served by a rationalist philosophy of science that posits the world in universal terms? According to whose logic are "objective" certainties of knowledge established? This feminist interrogation of objectivism soon gained currency in the social sciences, where the ethnocentric underpinnings of Western rationalism were further revealed. The answer to Harding's rhetorical question "Is science multicultural?" came back a resounding "no."[62] An important parallel to the feminist critique of objectivism emerged in analyses of language and representation. From such fundamental feminist issues as the critique of everyday speech emerged a more full-fledged inquiry into the role of linguistics in the development of thought and identity. Like objectivism, structuralist views of language offered a universal grammar in which rules and characteristics remain consistent from culture to culture. Also like objectivism, the structuralist view was too broad as a way of understanding how meaning functions. The feminist critique of this singular world view was soon adapted by visual theorists like Laura Mulvey and Teresa De Lauretis, who analyzed ways that media function as "technologies of gender."[63]

In the poststructuralist strain of this thinking, theorists questioned singular definitions of progress and rationality.[64] Michel Foucault, in particular, gained prominence in describing the "technologies of power" embedded in social institutions or such metaphorical constructs as the panopticon.[65] Although celebrated for their novelty, Foucault's views on technology can be seen as extensions of prior critiques of technocratic systems. For Foucault, such systems create environments within which people are controlled, often unwittingly. Yet Foucault departs from earlier analyses in his acknowledgement of the partial or contingent role played by technology in the context of other influences. Perhaps the most significant element in Foucault's formulation lies in the allowances he makes for human agency to resist or subvert "regimes of domination" in productive terms.

The post-structuralist critique of science and technology also is significant in its eschewal of essentialism. Many early determinist and substantive views, as well as their critiques by Marxists and feminists, constructed technology as an unchanging phenomenon that carried the same characteristics across time and space. In viewing technology as a contingent entity that functions differently in various contexts, post-structuralism suggests that technology is not necessarily a linear and unstoppable force. This leaves open the possibility for a view of technology as progressive, hence yielding a critical space in which to engage its problems and potentials.

To Feenberg, this dialectical view holds importance in its critical tolerance for rationality. Like it or not, rationalist objectivism holds a solid lock on the real-life discourses of science, jurisprudence, and education, to name a few. As Feenberg writes,

> Whatever the ultimate status of scientific-technical knowledge, it is what we use for truth in making policy. We need far more specific arguments against technocracy that can play at that level. Furthermore, it is implausible to dismiss rationality as merely a Western myth and to flatten all distinctions which so obviously differentiate modern from premodern society. There is something special captured in notions such as modernization, rationalization, and reification.[66]

As we recognize the problems with universal claims of "truth," the need persists for provisional or local truths that can be used in communication. This is where everyday culture comes in. The task of making meaning in each and every encounter is more complex and labor intensive, but it also promises that differences will not be elided as a matter of course. All of these issues have assumed a greater complexity in recent years, with the introduction of accessible technology in the form of home computers and network interfaces. Formerly abstract ideas about the role of technology in everyday life have become a part of daily existence.

Notes

1. Bureau of Labor Statistics, "American Time Use Summary," in *News* (Washington, DC: U.S. Department of Labor, 2005).

2. Elizabeth Thoman and Tessa Jolls, *Media Literacy: A National Priority for a Changing World*. *http://www.medialit.org/reading_room/article663.html*. Accessed May 10, 2005.

3. Ibid.

4. Howard Gardner, *Intelligence Reframed: Multiple Intelligences for the 21st Century* (New York: Basic Books, 1999), 10.

5. "Trivium," in *Wikipedia*, Jan. 22, 2007. *http://en.wikipedia.org/wiki/Trivium*. Accessed Jan. 22, 2007.

6. Neil Postman, *Amusing Ourselves to Death: Public Discourse in the Age of Show Business* (New York: Penguin Books, 1984), 44.

7. Ibid., 67.

8. Ibid.

9. Ibid., 25.

10. Ibid., 24–25.

11. Ibid., 72.

12. Ibid., 72–73.

13. Susan Sontag, *On Photography* (New York: Farrar, Straus, Giroux, 1977), 20.

14. Robert M. Diamond, "Single Room Television," in *A Guide to Instructional Media,* ed. Robert M. Diamond (New York: McGraw-Hill, 1964), 3.

15. John M. Hofstrand, "Television and Classroom Observation," in *A Guide to Instructional Media,* 149.

16. Marshall McLuhan, *Understanding Media: Extensions of Man* (New York: McGraw-Hill, 1964), 23.

17. The terms "visual literacy" and "media literacy" have been employed in a variety of differing contexts during the past two decades. The formalist media literacy of the 1970s should not be confused with the critical media literacy movement of the 1980s and 1990s.

18. Linda R. Burnett and Frederick Goldman, *Need Johnny Read? Practical Methods to Enrich Humanities Courses Using Films and Film Studies* (Dayton: Pflaum, 1971), xv.

19. Cary Bazalgette, as quoted in Ben Moore, "Media Education," in *The Media Studies Book* (New York: Routledge, 1991), 172.

20. Stanley Fish, *Is There a Text in this Class? The Authority of Interpretive Communities* (Cambridge: Harvard University Press, 1980).

21. Seymour Feshbach and Robert B. Singer, *Television and Aggression* (New York: Jossey-Bass, 1971), 12.

22. Concerns over the degrading effects of gritty printed material can be dated to the early decades of the nineteenth century. The introduction of plate lithography in 1801 made possible the mass production of books, pamphlets, and broadsides. In the United States, *The National Police Gazette,* first published in 1833, arose to satisfy the public hunger for stories of violent crime. History has demonstrated that periodic "moral panics" over media seem to parallel the development of new communication technologies and the social changes they enable. The Guttenberg press and the lithography process made possible dramatic leaps in the dissemination of written works. Both technologies allowed ordinary people access to what had formerly been available only to the privileged. And it made the elites nervous. This was certainly true in the mid-1800s, when commentators began to link social problems of the industrial era to emerging forms of popular media, often evoking images of an idealized past free

of such difficulty. Modernity had created a new working class of factory laborers often living in overcrowded urban tenements and hungry for the diversion provided by dime novels, newspapers, and vaudeville-type shows pandering to tastes for lust and violence. An English critic writing in 1851 described "one powerful agent for depraving the boyish classes of our population in our towns and cities is to be found in the cheap concerts, shows and theatres" that become "training schools of the coarsest and most open vice and filthiness." (Graham Murdock, "Reservoirs of Dogma: An Archaeology of Popular Anxieties," in *Ill Effects: The Media/Violence Debate,* eds. Martin Barker and Julia Petley [London and New York: Routledge, 1997], 152). According to Murdock, such sentiments typified a bourgeois fear of a growing working class of adolescent "hooligans" in need of policing. Like current formulations of an epidemic of violence in the media from which children needed inoculation, nineteenth century media critics like Frank Lydston wrote of a "psychic contagion in certain books that is as definite and disastrous as that of the plague. The germs of mental ill health are as potent in their way and ... as far reaching in evil effects as syphilis or leprosy." (Murdock, 160). Nineteenth-century modernism grew fond of expressing social concern in scientific terms, with medical metaphors deployed in many contexts. Drawing on terminology of germ theory and epidemiology, writers discussing poverty spoke of infections, contagions, and plague spots within impoverished communities. (Paul Boyer, "Building Character Among the Urban Poor," in *Social Welfare Policy,* ed. Ira Colby [Chicago: Dorsey Press, 1989], 113–134). To Herbert Spencer, such sickness was a necessary part of social evolution: "Having, by unwise institutions brought into existence large numbers who are unadapted to the requirements of social life, and are consequently sources of misery to themselves and others, we cannot repress and gradually diminish this body of relatively worthless people without inflicting much pain. Evil has been done and the penalty must be paid. Cure can only come through affliction." (Herbert Spencer, *The Principles of Ethics, Vol. 1* (New York: Appleton & Co., 1904).

23. Senate Committee on the Judiciary, Children, Violence, and the Media: A Report for Parents and Policy Makers, September 14, 1999.

24. Realvision, *Facts and Figures About Our TV Habit.* http://www. *chamisamesa.net/tvoff.html.* Accessed May 2, 2005.

25. Ibid.

26. National Television Violence Study, "Executive Summary," *NTVS Brochure* (1998), 8. *http://www.ccsp.ucsb.edu/execsum.pdf.* Accessed May 21, 2005.

27. Karl Lorenz, *On Aggression* (New York: Harcourt Brace and World, 1963).

28. George Gerbner, et. al, "Growing Up with Television: The Cultivation Perspective," in *Media Effects: Advances in Theory and Research,* 2nd edition, eds. J. Bryant and Dolf Zillman (Hillsdale, NJ: Lawrence Earlbaum, 2002).

29. Harold Schechter, *Savage Pastimes: A Cultural History of Violent Entertainment* (New York: St. Martin's Press, 2005), 122.

30. The invention of photography in the mid-1800s made the production of moving pictures possible by the turn of the century. Violence was the centerpiece of early movies. Thomas Edison demonstrated the new technology in 1895 with his Kinetoscope film *The Execution of Mary, Queen of Scots,* a thirty-second clip of a beheading. Movies of boxing matches proved to be a sensation. The immediate success of *The Corbett-Fitzsimmons Fight* (1896) gave it the dubious distinction of being one of the first films to evoke the ire of antimedia violence critics, a sentiment that led to a ban of prizefighting movies in 1912. Like today's effects-laden action films, graphic depictions in movies like Sigmund Lubin's *Chinese Massacring Christians* (1900) or George Mêlées *The Last Days of Anne Boleyn* (1905) were used to help show off the features of the moving image. Early movies were especially popular among the new immigrant populations emerging in urban centers. The visual language of film made proficiency in English irrelevant to these audiences. Soon local lawmakers and social reformers grew concerned over the perceived risks of exposing the ethnic working class and the young to such fare. When New York City Mayor George McClennan ordered moving picture exhibition licenses revoked in 1908, a group of theater companies (including Biograph, Lowe, Edison, and Pathé), founded by the National Board of Review (NBR). As

the entertainment industry would do again in later decades, this gesture of self-regulation served to preempt government intervention in movie content. The NBR passed moral judgments on films, failing those that glorified crime or that it believed presented excessive "suffering, brutality, vulgarity, or violence." (J. David Slocum, "Introduction: Violence and American Cinema: Notes for an Investigation," in *Violence and American Cinema,* ed. J. David Slocum (New York and London: Routledge, 2001), 5). Approved films often ran the legend "Passed by the National Board of Review" in their title sequences. The regulation of movies took place in the context of more generalized concerns over public morality and the productivity of the national workforce. Such thinking led to the 1919 passage of the Eighteenth Amendment prohibiting the manufacture and sale of alcohol, which remained in effect until repealed by Congress in 1933.In 1922, film production companies formed their own regulatory organization, the Motion Picture Producers and Distributors Association of America (MPPDA), which established standards of appropriate content. The MPPDA was led famously by Will Hays, who for two decades was recognized by the American public as the nation's "movie czar." The MPPDA efforts led to the establishment of the film industry's Production Code, codifying content guidelines. Recognizing that movies "may be directly responsible for spiritual or moral progress, for higher types of social life, and for much correct thinking," the Production Code, which remained a governing force in moviemaking from 1930 to 1958, deemed inappropriate depictions of such practices as murder, brutal killing, safecracking, the dynamiting of trains, adultery, lustful kissing, or miscegenation (Motion Picture Producers and Distributors of America [MPPDA], *The Motion Picture Code of 1930* [Hays Code], *http://www.ArtsReformation.com.* Accessed May 26, 2005). Bolstering these views were the findings of the influential Payne Fund Studies conducted in the late 1920s. Surveying the attitudes of students and young adult office workers, the Payne Fund concluded that "motion pictures are a genuine educational institution; not educational in the restricted and conventional sense ... but educational in the truer sense of actually introducing [viewers] to a type of life which has immediate, practical, and momentous significance." (Herbert

Blummer, *Movies and Conduct* [New York: Macmillan, 1933], 200). Although conducted with research subjects described as adolescents, the study framed its findings on "the great influence of motion pictures on the play of children" as "a source for considerable imitation," characterizing children as "blank slates." (Blummer, 192).This extrapolation from the observation of children would become a template for most discussions of media violence for the rest of the century. Together with the Production Code, the Payne Fund Studies succeeded in sanitizing most motion picture production through the 1960s. The only movies that escaped such regulation of violence were World War II–era newsreels.With the end of the Second World War, public concern in the United States shifted to domestic well-being. The newly emergent suburban middle-class sought safety and often settled for conformity, while seeking to avoid threats of any kind. Attention focused on the perceived dangers posed by undisciplined young people, immigrant populations, communists, and the growing popularity of violent Westerns and crime movies. A senate investigation launched by Estes Kefauver in 1950 concluded that comic books contributed to juvenile crime rates. Like the infamous McCarthy hearings of the same period that persecuted perceived communists, the Kefauver proceedings sought to prove a connection between crime and immigrant groups, primarily focusing on the Italian mafia. Within a few years other media became targets of the Kefauver Committee by association, with the genre of teenage film blamed for making young people insensitive to crime, death, and pain. Prompted again to act in the interest of avoiding government regulation, the film industry in 1956 enacted a voluntary moratorium on the production of "juvenile delinquency" films like *The Wild One* (1953) and *Rebel Without a Cause* (1955).

31.   UC–Santa Barbara Center for Communication and Social Policy, "Year 3 Executive Summary," in *National Television Violence Study (NTVS)* (1998). *http://www.ccsp.ucsb.edu/execsum.pdf*. Accessed. Oct. 8, 2005.

32.   American Academy of Pediatrics (AAP) and American Academy of Child and Adolescent Psychiatry (AACAP), "Media Violence Harms Children" from *American Academy of Pediatrics and the American Academy of Child and Adolescent Psychiatry's Joint Statement on the Impact of*

Entertainment Violence on Children—Congressional Public Health Summit, July 26, 2000 (New York: Lippincott, Williams, and Wilkins, 2000).

33. Ibid.

34. American Psychological Association, as cited in *Is Media Violence a Problem?* ed. James D. Torr (San Diego: Greenhaven, 2000), 6.

35. Ibid., 7.

36. National Center for Missing and Exploited Children, "FAQs and Stastistics," *http://www.missingkids.com/*. Accessed. Oct. 10, 2005.

37. J. J. Pilotta, D. E. Schultz, G. Drenik, and P. Rist, "Simultaneous Media Usage Study (SIMM)," *Journal of Consumer Behavior* (2004).

38. The AAP is one of a number of professional organizations that have claimed for years that studies have shown media violence to cause violent behavior. But as the letter to the AAP says, "Correlations between aggressive behavior and preference for violent entertainment do not demonstrate that one causes the other. Laboratory experiments that are designed to test causation rely on substitutes for aggression, some quite farfetched. Punching Bobo dolls, pushing buzzers, and recognizing 'aggressive words' on a computer screen are all a far cry from real-world aggression." Researchers have also manipulated data to achieve "statistically significant" results. This issue of scientific accuracy is important, say those writing, because the "unending political crusades on this issue, abetted by professional organizations like AAP, have crowded out discussion of proven health dangers to kids, such as child abuse, child poverty, and family violence. This may make our politicians happy, but we should expect more of physicians." Those signing the letter included: Professor Jib Fowles, University of Houston; Professor Henry Giroux, Pennsylvania State University; Professor Jeffrey Goldstein, University of Utrecht, The Netherlands; Professor Robert Horwitz, University of California–San Diego; Professor Henry Jenkins, Massachusetts Institute of Technology; Professor Vivian Sobchack, University of California–Los Angeles; Michael Males, Justice Policy Institute, Center on Juvenile and Criminal Justice; and Richard Rhodes, science historian and Pulitzer Prize laureate. The letter was also signed by Marjorie Heins, director of the Free Expression Policy Project at the National Coalition Against Censorship; Christopher

Finan, director of the American Booksellers Foundation for Free Expression; and David Greene, director of the Oakland, California–based First Amendment Project. See "Scholars Ask American Academy of Pediatrics to Reconsider Misstatements about Media Violence," Free Expression Network, Dec. 5, 2001 *http://www.freeexpression.org/newswire/1205_2001. htm* Accessed June 2, 2005.

39. James Gee, *What Video Games Have to Teach Us About Literacy and Learning* (New York: Palgrave, 2003).

40. Steven Johnson, *Everything Bad Is Good for You: How Today's Popular Culture Is Actually Making Us Smarter* (New York: Riverhead, 2005).

41. Stephen Prince, *Screening Violence* (New Brunswick, NJ: Rutgers, 2000), 187.

42. David Levi Strauss, *Between the Eyes: Essays on Photography and Politics* (New York: Aperture, 2003), 81.

43. Levi Strauss, 91.

44. Lynn Hirschberg, "Giving Them What They Want," in *New York Times Magazine,* Sept. 4, 2005, 32.

45. Sam Peckinpah quoted by Steven Prince, "The Aesthetic of Slow-Motion Violence in the Films of Sam Peckinpah," in *Screening Violence* (New Brunswick, NJ: Rutgers University Press, 2003), 176.

46. Entertainment Software Association, *Facts and Research: Game Player Data* (2005). *http://www.theesa.com/facts/gamer–data.php.* Accessed May 3, 2005.

47. Media Awareness Network, *The Business of Media Violence.* *http://www.media-awareness.ca.* Accessed May 3, 2005.

48. Entertainment Software Association, *Facts and Research: Game Player Data. http://www.theesa.com/facts/gamer_data.php.* Accessed Oct. 5, 2005.

49. Tor Thoresen, "NPD Paints Mixed Picture of Games in 2005," *Gamespot News,* Jan. 18, 2006. *http://www.gamespot.com/news/6142571. html.* Accessed April 2, 2006.

50. Amy Goodman and David Goodman, "Why Media Ownership Matters," *The Seattle Times,* April 3, 2005. *http://seattletimes.nwsource.*

com/html/opinion/2002228040_sundaygoodman03.html. Accessed Aug. 2, 2005.

51. Richard Coyne, *Technoromanticism: Digital Narrative, Holism, and the Romance of the Real* (Cambridge: MIT Press, 1999). Citing Martin Plattel and others, Coyne presents a detailed discussion of the way utopian narratives reflect social anxieties.

52. Jeremy Rifkin, *The Age of Access: The New Culture of Hypercapitalism, Where All of Life Is a Paid-for Experience* (New York: Putnam, 2000), 173.

53. Martin Heidegger, *The Question of Technology,* trans. William Lovitt (New York: Harper and Row, 1977).

54. Leo Marx, "The Idea of Technology and Postmodern Pessimism," in *Technology, Pessimism, and Postmodernism,* eds. Yaron Ezrahi, Everett Mendleson, and Howard P. Segal (Amherst: University of Massachusetts Press, 1995), 14.

55. Ibid.

56. Marx in *Technology, Pessimism, and Postmodernism,* 19.

57. Andrew Feenberg, *Critical Theory of Technology* (New York: Oxford University Press, 1991); Andrew Feenberg and Alastair Hannay, eds., *Technology and the Politics of Knowledge* (Bloomington and Indianapolis: Indiana University Press, 1995); Andrew Feenberg, *Questioning Technology* (New York and London: Routledge, 1998).

58. Martin Heidegger, *Being and Time,* trans. John Macquarrie and Edward Robinson (New York: Harper and Row, 1962), 41.

59. Jacques Ellul, *The Technological System,* trans. Joachim Neugroschel (New York: Continuum, 1980).

60. Andrew Ross, *Strange Weather: Culture, Science, and Technology in the Age of Limits* (London: Verso, 1991), 10.

61. Ibid.

62. Sandra Harding, *Is Science Multicultural? Postcolonialisms, Feminisms, Epistemologies* (Bloomington and Indianapolis: University of Indiana, 1998).

63. Laura Mulvey, *Visual and Other Pleasures* (Bloomington: Indiana University Press, 1989); Teresa De Lauretis, *Technologies of Gender:*

Essays on Theory, Film, and Fiction (Bloomington: Indiana University Press, 1987).

64. See Ezrahi, Mendelsohn, and Segal, eds., *Technology, Pessimism, and Postmodernism*.

65. Michel Foucault, *Discipline and Punishment*, trans. Asheridan (New York: Pantheon, 1977).

66. Arthur Kroker and Michael A. Weinstein, *Data Trash: The Theory of the Virtual Class* (New York: Plagrave, 1994), 4.

Chapter Four
Finding

Self and Identity

This chapter of *Everyday Culture* addresses issues of self-discovery and the individual, asking such questions as these: Who do you think you are? What are the circumstances and forces that shape self-concept? What forms of learning inform our understandings of ourselves? How are we different from one another? How do we form our opinions? Do outside entities make efforts to influence our beliefs? How can we be more informed and critical about acting in our interests? What can we do to express our wants and take action to make the world a better place?

One of the primary ways we know ourselves and others know us is through the linguistic labeling of naming. Language plays an enormous role in the way we come to know the world. Some say that it is only through "representations" of various languages and sign systems that we come to know anything. Very early in life language helps people understand the ways they resemble and differ from others, how they fit in and are excluded from various groupings, and how society and the world are organized.

The first essay in this chapter, "Self and Naming," looks at ways that language influences the formation of self-concept, specifically as it relates to what individuals and groups call themselves and are called by others. The next essay, "Difference," addresses self and identity by examining how we are both similar and different from one another. How do these attributes influence how we form our opinions? Do outside entities make efforts to influence our beliefs? How can we become more informed and critical about acting in our interests? What can we do to express our wants and take action to make the world a better place? The third section, "Unstable Meanings," discusses how peoples' views of themselves and the world can change. The last essay, "Fear, Ethics, and Everyday Life," discusses the role of communication technologies in shaping our perceptions of threat and danger in our lives. The essay asks whether continual exposure to fear-producing images can change a person's worldview, behavior, and identity.

Self and Naming

Names help in finding the way. They help us find ourselves and help others find us—and they tell about where we came from and where we want to go. Individuals' given names can describe personal genealogy, ethnicity, and religion, as well as family transformations and journeys. When parents name their children they often make conscious or unconscious statements about their own identities, hopes, and aspirations—just as adults do who choose to adopt new names, create hyphenated combinations, or simply use a nickname. Generations of immigrants coming to the United States chose to alter first or last names in gestures of assimilation. Just as frequently, people have honored their nations of origin by adopting traditional names. While many women (and some men) change their names when they marry, others don't. Such decisions can be fraught with emotion, cultural implications, and even political beliefs. In her book *Mixed Blessings,* critic Lucy Lippard devotes a chapter to the topic of naming. Lippard begins by observing that

> For better or worse, social existence is predicated on names. Names and labels are at once the most private and most public words in the life of an individual or a group. For all their apparent permanence, they are susceptible to the winds of both personal and political change. Naming is the active tense of identity, the outward aspect of the self-representation process, acknowledging all the circumstances through which it must elbow its way.[1]

Consider the names that celebrities have given themselves. Michael Caine was born Maurice Micklewhite, and Cat Stevens is now Yusef Islam. Other celebrities and their original names include: Bono (Paul Hewson), Vin Diesel (Mark Vincent), 50 Cent (Martin Kelvin), Eminem (Marshall Mathers), Mos Def (Dante Smith), Ice T (Tracy Marrow), and Carole King (Carole Klein). Motives vary for celebrity renaming, including efforts to add distinction, simplify pronunciation, and neutralize or accentuate ethnicity.

One indication of national tastes and attitudes resides in the names given to children. In 2006 the U.S. Census Bureau reported the top five names for boys to be Jacob, Michael, Joshua, Matthew, and Ethan. For girls the top names were Emily, Emma, Madison, Abigail, and Olivia. Of these ten names only Michael appeared in the top twenty in 1976, when David, Christopher, Jennifer, and Amy led the lists. In recent years, growing attention has focused on the increasingly unusual names that performers are giving their offspring. Comedian Penn Gillette's daughter is named Moxie Crimefighter, Gwyneth Paltrow and Chris Martin chose Apple for their daughter, Rachel Griffiths selected Banjo for her son, Bruce

Willis and Demi Moore named their child Scout. Notable clusters of names include those chosen by Bob Geldof for his girls, Peaches, Trixie, and Fifi Trixibelle—and Robert Rodriguez calling his sons Rebel, Racer, Rocket, and Rogue.

Group names are just as complex and charged with emotion, especially when referring to race or ethnicity. Lippard suggests that three kinds of naming get applied to groups: *self-naming, external labeling,* and *racist name-calling.*

Self-naming denotes the terms and definitions that members of a group use for themselves, ranging from the traditional to the ironic or comic. As so-called minority groups within the United States have become more politicized and activist-oriented on this issue of names, self-naming has involved taking control over what a group is called. In the course of the twentieth century, "colored people" became Negros, then blacks, Afro-Americans, African Americans, and eventually people of color, with each transition marked by social and political foment. Other groups have followed similar trajectories of self-naming. Sometimes the process can be confusing to those outside the self-naming culture. Being Asian American is not the same as being Asian in America. Equally complicated is the ironic use or appropriation of negative terminology, as when rappers use variations of the infamous "n-word," or other groups put new spins on derisive terms. As Lippard writes, "Self-naming is a project in which such relational factors—balancing one's own assumptions with an understanding of others—are all-important. When names and labels prove insubstantial or damaging, they can of course be exposed as falsely engendered and socially constructed by those who experience them; they can be discarded and discredited. But they can also be chosen anew."[2]

External labeling occurs when one group is named by another in supposedly neutral terms. Often this external labeling results in inaccuracies in names like Hispanic, Oriental, or American Indian that generalize about groups and often minimize diverse histories, languages, or memberships. At other times, external naming can seem nearly indistinguishable from racist name-calling. Native American nicknames and mascots can be seen everywhere in our society. People drive Jeep Cherokees, watch Atlanta Braves baseball fans do the tomahawk chop, and support football teams such as the Kansas City Chiefs and the Florida State University Seminoles. Are the uses of these symbols a tribute to the Native American people or, as some feel, a slap in the face to their honored traditions? In April 2001, the U.S. Commission on Civil Rights recommended that all non–Native American schools drop their Native American mascots or nicknames. The commission declared that "the stereotyping of any racial, ethnic, religious or other group, when promoted by our public educational institutions, teaches all students that stereotyping of minority groups is acceptable, which is a dangerous lesson in a diverse society."[3] The commission also noted that these nicknames and mascots are "false portrayals that encourage biases and prejudices that have a negative effect on contemporary Indian people."[4]

Racist name-calling requires little explanation. It often reflects more on the ignorance, bigotry, or fear of the name-caller than anyone to whom or about whom an epithet is directed. Among the terms used in the Unites States that Wikipedia lists under "Ethnic Slurs" are the following: Bagel Dog (Jewish), Beaner (Chicano/Latino), Bin-Laden (Arab), Boater (Asian), Buckwheat (African American), Boris (Russian), Cracker (U.S. Caucasian), Dago (Italian), Dim Sum (Chinese), Dog

Eater (Filipino/Vietnamese), Donkey (Irish), Fisheye (U.S. Caucasian), Frog (French), Gandhi (Indian), Guido (Italian), Honkey (U.S. Caucasian), Kraut (German), Leprechaun (Irish), Kike (Jew), Mo (Muslim), Nip (Japanese), Paddy (Irish), Pedro (Mexican), Pineapple (Hawaiian), Polly (Polynesian), Pork Chop (Portuguese), Push Start (South Asian), Redskin (U.S. Indigenous), Sambo (African American), Skunk (Middle Eastern), Slant-Eye (Asian), Slob (Russian), Snail Eater (French), Space (African American), Spaghetti (Italian), Towelhead (Muslim, Sikh), Whitey (U.S. Caucasian), and Wop (Italian). As part of vernacular language, new slurs are continually appearing, making the practice of antiracism a continuing concern.

Naming is an extension of language. Like the control that comes with self-naming, facility with language affords speakers the ability to shape representations in the world and to exert their will by speaking in that world. This may not seem that significant for people living in a nation where their native language is spoken. But for individuals who immigrate or for those from nations where an external language was imposed, issues of what language is spoken and by whom carry serious implications. Most people recognize that literacy is a key to success in employment, school, and communicating for something as mundane as applying for a driver's license. As artist Jimmie Durham states, "Indian people still speak English as a second language, even if we no longer speak our own languages. That is the true meaning of illiteracy in a class society; one is not in control of the language one speaks."[5]

In the colonial era, England, France, and Spain (among numerous others) imposed their languages on the nations they colonized. Such acts of linguistic control made explicit the military and economic domination that colonizers exerted over the nations they subjugated. In India, Hong Kong, and numerous African colonies, the British justified the imposition of their language on the basis of efficiency and political expedience. Not only would one language simplify communication in commerce and government, but a single imposed language might eradicate antagonisms within regions where numerous native languages and dialects existed. Rarely did the process of linguistic reconfiguration go smoothly. Yet in nations like India the process eventually made facility in English synonymous with upward mobility and success. Today, there are 350 million English-language speakers in India—more than the combined populations of Britain and the United States. Not that everyone is pleased with this outcome. To many, the long imposition of English culture has meant a devaluing of preexisting regional culture and a loss of self-respect. This issue of cultural devaluation is succinctly articulated in a videotape by artist Meena Nanji entitled *It Is a Crime* (1997). The videotape connects the issue of spoken/written English with filmic representations and stereotypes generated by English and American media. The tape presents a montage of Indian men as crazed mystics, Indian women as voluptuous temptresses, and the nation of India itself as an exotic tourist destination. The tape takes its name from a poem by Shanti Mootoo, which also provides a script that is projected over the film footage. The first line reads: "It is a crime that I should have to use your language to tell you how I feel that you have taken mine from me."

Similar disputes over linguistic representation are manifest in U.S. hip-hop culture and its musical subgenre, rap. Clearly, naming is important, indicated by the number of performers who have amended or replaced their names with designations that reflect issues of community or cultural heritage—or that simply serve as description, homage, comedy, statement of solidarity, or rebellious expression. When rap and hip-hop artists adopt names, they are often making explicit statements about themselves and their communities. Tupac Shakur retained the last name of his mother, Black Panther Revolutionary Party member Afeni Shakur. To this he added the name Tupac Amaru from a sixteenth-century Incan chief whose name means "shining serpent." Executed in 1572, Tupac Amaru was the last Incan leader to be defeated by the Spanish. The Tupac Amaru Revolutionary Movement led by Nestor Cerpa Cartolini was active in Peru during Tupac Shakur's lifetime and its oppositional activities remained an inspiration to him.

Shakur's last name also was adopted, but by his mother and stepfather. Tupac's mother, Afeni Shakur, was a single parent when she raised her son, a task Tupac valorized in his song "Dear Mama." Struggling with a dependence on crack cocaine, Afeni Shakur—born Alice Faye Williams—was imprisoned while pregnant with Tupac for withholding information pertaining to a trial of Black Panther leaders. Eventually acquitted, Afeni married Mutulu Shakur after Tupac was born. Mutulu Shakur's given name had been Jeral Wayne Williams. An acupuncturist and black revolutionary, Mutulu was convicted of attempting to free from prison Tupac's "aunt" Joanne Chesinard, who later changed her name to Assata Shakur.[6] In Mutulu's absence, Tupac acquired a second paternal influence in his godfather, Elmer "Geronimo" Pratt, also known as Geronimo ji-Jaga, a high-ranking member of the Black Panthers. All of these figures in Tupac's upbringing changed their names to publicly mark themselves as adherents to the doctrines of self-defense and class rebellion that lay at the heart of the Black Panther movement. In doing so, they gave testimony to the enduring importance of names—and specifically to the importance of naming in African American culture.

"A good name," wrote Spanish author Miguel Cervantes, "is better than riches." In many parts of Africa, when children are born they traditionally are given names that reflect the circumstances surrounding their birth or names that describe their communities or the hopes their parents hold for them. The slaves brought to the United States two hundred years ago often were stripped of the names they were given in their native countries, an act that for many destroyed a vital link to their nations of origin and erased their cultural heritage. Rather than being called by their original and often very beautiful given names, African slaves received new names from the Bible (the first man and woman slave brought upon each ship often were named Adam and Eve), or short, simple names (like Jack or Tom), or nicknames. At the end of the Civil War in 1865 many slaves changed their names to reflect newly won freedom by changing the spelling of their names or giving themselves last names. But very few of them reverted to their ancestral African names because those names had been forgotten in the generations since their grandparents or great-grandparents had been brought to the United States. Prevailing racial bias also discouraged many African Americans from adopting African names. The civil rights movement of the 1950s and 1960s brought with it an interest in the history of slavery and encouraged many African Americans to resurrect their cultural heritage. Traditional African names and names from the Muslim religion began appearing with growing frequency. Civil rights leader Stokely Carmichael changed his name to Kwame Touré by adopting the first name of one African leader and the last name of another. Malcolm Little (later known as Malcolm X) and his wife Betty Jean Sanders changed their last name to Shabazz.

Naming and the manipulation of language are key elements in rap music and hip-hop culture. Writer bell hooks states that "rap music provides a public voice for young black men who are usually silenced and overlooked. It emerged in the streets outside the confines of a domesticity shaped and informed by poverty, outside enclosed spaces where ... [black bodies] ... had to be contained and controlled."[7] On the other hand, artist Chuck D famously referred to rap as the "CNN of black people." In this sense, rap has been considered by many as a straightforward description of African American life as much as an incitement or protest. Or is rap better understood as a product of history and tradition? Musical scholars will cite the roots of rap that extend back to idioms like jazz, blues, and even reggae. At the other extreme, some contemporary critics emphasize rap's articulation of postmodern theories of appropriation and bricolage. Like many contemporary visual artists, rap performers often borrow, quote, or otherwise comment upon lyrics, melodies, or recorded elements of music from others. Or is rap really best understood in political terms? Much rap directly confronts white power structures and institutions of discrimination that have plagued the black community in the United States for two hundred years. In this vein, some have compared the revolutionary message of rap to activist groups of the 1960s and 1970s such as the Black Panthers and the Student Nonviolent Coordinating Committee (SNCC), among others. Because of its revolutionary implications, some scholars have pointed out the important educational functions of rap as a vehicle of consciousness-raising. Peter McLaren includes among rap's idioms:

> Its fixing of "in-your-face" rhymes to social meltdown and bass rhythms to urban disaster; its commodification of black rage through high-volume and low-frequency sound; its production of sexualizing fugues for an imploding Generation X . . . its production of affective economies of white panic around a generalized fear of a black planet; its sneering, tongue-flicking contempt of public space; its visceral intensity and corporal immediacy; its snarling, subterranean resistance; its eschatological showdown of "us" against "them"; its "edutainers" down with the brothas in the street; its misogynist braggadocio; its pimp-

inspired subjectivity; its urban war zone counternarratives.[8]

Some have compared hip-hop artists with "knowledge warriors" of the kind that Antonio Gramsci was describing in his formulation of the organic intellectual. Gramsci valorized the efforts of those informally schooled thinkers who arose from ranks of ordinary people to assist in the self-actualization of the masses. This is not to suggest that all views of rap are so heroic. The famous sexism of many rap lyrics, the materialism of its performers, and the implicit endorsement of gang violence—these also need to be included in any collection of rap definitions, as does that enormous economic force that rap represents within the commercial music and entertainment industries.

Difference

Difference as a Problem or an Asset

Many of the most commonly heard arguments over the everyday stem from differing attitudes toward cultural sameness and difference. Those believing difference to constitute a problem assert that society should be working toward a common set of beliefs and standards, with the assumption that cultural sameness is the basis for social coherence, stability, and the minimization of disagreements. From this perspective, society needs common laws, common values, a single language, and shared cultural icons. Proponents of sameness see difference as a problem and they assert that social coherence depends on a firm set of standards to which everyone should subscribe. Outsiders need to adopt the majority view through a process known as assimilation. Assimilationists often assert that their nation has achieved its present state of development as a consequence of its ability to forge a single, unified, national identity. Assimilationists claim that separating citizens by such categories as ethnicity, race, or religion—and providing immigrant groups "special privileges"—can harm the very groups they seek to assist. By highlighting differences between these groups and the majority in this way, the government may foster resentment towards them by the majority. This makes the immigrant group resist mainstream culture. Assimilationists suggest that if a society makes a full effort to incorporate immigrants into the mainstream, immigrants will then naturally work to reciprocate the gesture and adopt new customs. Through this process, it is argued, national unity is retained. The assimilationist view has held sway in most school programs, and it is the attitude conservatives now press in the cultural realm. Its ethos dates to the early days of the republic, as typified in the words of eighteenth century French immigrant Hector St. John de Crevecoeur: "He is American, who, leaving behind him all his ancient prejudices and manners, receives new ones from the new mode of life he has embraced, the new government he obeys, and the new rank he holds. . . . Here individuals of all nations are melted into a new race of man."[9] From the reasonable assertion that social cohesion is formed through shared values and compromise, this position can deteriorate into a rigid extremism. The result is an ossified traditionalism that asserts a single culture over all others.

Proponents of cultural difference as an asset argue for a tolerance of diverse attitudes and ways of understanding the world, claiming that cultural difference is a source of social vitality, dynamism, and continual change. Supporters of cultural difference believe in valuing different perspectives. Within this logic people have different histories and they are inherently individualistic. Making everyone the same is tyrannical and antidemocratic. People don't need to surrender their identities. Difference is good for society and variety is a healthy attribute. Different people need different amounts and kinds of resources. The privileging of difference as an asset can evolve into an attitude known as separatism. Reacting against the oppressive implications of assimilation, separatist groups move to consolidate constituent identity. For example, separatism in educational curricula replaces dominant knowledge with group-specific knowledge. This can imply exclusive relationships to domains of knowledge based on social location. Such an attitude refutes the presumption that anyone can possess an adequate knowledge of the needs and placement of other groups.

Difference and Cultural Standards

The idea that members of a society should share the same beliefs and values in the interest of social coherence lies beneath such hot-button issues as gay marriage, reproductive rights, prayer in schools, immigrant rights, the English-only movement, decency in the media, and arts censorship. Proponents of sameness in society argue certain values and beliefs have emerged from tradition because they are inherently superior to others. These values and beliefs are therefore asserted to be natural and correct, representing what is normal and "good" for society. Within this scheme, people falling outside prescribed definitions of normalcy are required to change themselves and adopt the principles of the social mainstream. These issues can erupt in dramatic emotionalism as when, for example, conservative Representative Richard Santorum declared in 2006 that gay marriage threatened to undermine the institution of the American family. "It threatens my marriage, it threatens all marriages," Santorum said to the *New York Times*.[10] Santorum's statement might seem illogical, since by most estimates gays and lesbians account for less than ten percent of the population. But to Santorum and those like him, belief systems that support only heterosexual marriage need constant protection. The cause was endorsed later in the year by President George W. Bush, who backed a resolution to amend the U.S. Constitution to define marriage as a union between a man and a woman. "Ages of experience have taught us that the commitment of a husband and a wife to love and to serve one another promotes the welfare of children and the stability of society," Bush said.[11] "Marriage cannot be cut off from its cultural, religious, and natural roots without weakening this good influence on society."[12] The same desire for cultural homogeneity lies behind efforts to criminalize abortion, legislate prayer in all schools, and clamp down on immigration.

The problem isn't whether one agrees or disagrees with one side or another on these issues. It has to do with the fact that in a democracy disagreement is supposedly permitted so that people are allowed to live together with different views on issues and with different attitudes toward how they live their lives. What is normal or correct to one group of people may not be so to another. Besides, many kinds of differences shouldn't or can't be changed. Historically, American society has maintained a commitment to values of tolerance, individual liberty, a diversity of opinion. As a nation primarily composed of immigrants who have come to the "new world" over the past three centuries, Americans constitute a heterogeneous people. This diversity contributes to complexity and ultimately to the intelligence of our society. Newcomers bring fresh perspectives, new ways of looking at the world, and unforeseen approaches to solving problems. The diversity of these perspectives protects society from falling into narrow orthodoxies. This is partly what makes everyday experience so important. The everyday encounters and decisions people make allow them to follow or not follow a given way of thinking. Individuals can endorse a standard behavior, go their own way, or invent something entirely new to them. In other words, people can deviate.

Views of what society considers normal or deviant merit constant scrutiny and reevaluation. Sociologist Howard Becker wrote about this in his classic book about motorcycle gangs in the 1960s, *Outsiders*.[13] At the time, motorcycle gangs were considered the exemplification of social "deviance." Their members dressed strangely, broke rules, disrupted communities, lived dangerously, and sometimes committed crimes. In the academic world, sociologists looking strictly at gang behavior had difficulty coming up with prescriptions of what to do about the problem. According to Becker, social scientists at the time focused on the symptoms of deviance and "accepted the commonsense notion that there must be something wrong" with gang members, "otherwise they wouldn't act that way."[14] Becker's solution was to take a more contextual approach, looking at the broader social circumstances that made members of gangs perceive themselves as outsiders. He found that gang members often came from poor or working-class families, that they were offered little opportunities for education or employment, and that their life experiences had told them that following the standards of normal social behavior would give them little opportunity for happiness or success. In contrast, gang membership offered support, friendship, and social status within the gang, as well as a means of having pleasure and striking back against the oppressive authority of mainstream society. In many ways, outsider status seemed a logical preference given the social conditions from which its members emerged. In this context, what dominant society viewed as deviant was instead quite normal within the gang worldview. Becker concluded that "labeling gang members as outsiders to be ostracized and punished by mainstream society wasn't going to solve the problem of their perceived deviance. Rather than asking members of motorcycle gangs to change their attitudes, perhaps public policies might be adjusted to provide access to good schools, job opportunities, and ways to succeed. Findings like Becker's had profound implications in challenging what was termed "normative" sociology.[15] Along with other thinkers in the 1960s and 1970s, Becker helped bring about a recognition that views of morality and behavioral standards were relative to given societies and held in place by groups with power. Hence social norms determined by social majorities needed study and adjustment over time.

Multiculturalism

Multiculturalism has evolved into a term with diverse meanings and uses. Like most complex expressions, multiculturalism needs to be understood from both an historical and a conceptual perspective. The term came into common usage during the early 1980s in the context of public school curriculum reform. Multiculturalists argued that the content of classes in history, literature, and other areas reflected a Eurocentric bias—excluding people of color and groups from outside the Western European tradition—not to mention women. As Gregory Jay observes, "This material absence was also interpreted as a value judgment that reinforced unhealthy ethnocentric and even racist attitudes."[16] To Jay, "the historical event of multiculturalism brought with it many complicated conceptual problems, causing a rich debate over what multiculturalism is or should mean."[17] Most proponents of multiculturalism see it as a middle ground between extreme views of difference exclusively as an asset or problem. Multiculturalism also seeks to overcome simple "mainstream versus margin" dichotomies that would separate people into either/or categories of inclusion and exclusion. All too often groups seen as dominant are permitted to establish the parameters of the culture, the understood rules about how things are done in the group, whether that mainstream is a small subgroup or a majority within the group.

Those at the margins are obliged to adapt to what the mainstream sets up. Lost in such dynamics are the recognitions that a person can be mainstream one way and marginal in another way at the same time, depending on what characteristics one is looking at. If an individual is mainstream in a certain group, there are other groups in which that person falls to the margin. We all have experiences of being in the mainstream and being in the margin. In light of these dynamics, multiculturalists have brought attention to how deceptive the very term mainstream can be. When scrutinized carefully, the mythic mainstream promoted in the media excludes young and old people, rich and poor individuals, liberals and conservatives, people who belong to ethnic groups, students, retired people, gays and lesbians, divorced or single people, members of religious groups, and so on. Put another way, the so-called mainstream actually excludes the majority of people. It is a linguistic convention used to promote an illusion of common values and unproblemmatized unity. Although this imaginary mainstream purportedly includes a majority of people, it actually excludes everyone. Rather than functioning as a marker of the middle ground, it works as a mechanism to naturalize social hierarchies.

Another concept multiculturalists have challenged is the view of the United States as a melting pot, asserting that the melting pot metaphor is a cover for oppressive assimilation.[18] Multiculturalists assert that melting pot assimilation damages minority cultures by stripping away their distinctive features. With assimilation, immigrants lose their original cultural (and often linguistic) identities. This loss of culture is often systematized by institutions of the dominant culture (such as naturalization bureaus, schools, social organizations) that initiate programs to assimilate or integrate minority cultures. Although some multiculturalists admit that assimilation in the interest of cultural homogeneity may yield benefits such as cultural literacy or a sense of nationalistic belonging, negative effects also can result when minorities are strongly urged to assimilate, as when groups fiercely oppose integration. For example, immigrants who flee persecution or leave a country devastated by war understandably may be resistant to abandoning their heritage. For such reasons, many multiculturalists argue for the preservation of distinctly different ethnic, racial, or cultural communities without melting them into a common culture—especially when melting implies the erasure of immigrant cultures.

Multiculturalism also seeks to overcome practices of homogenization, which treat all members of a group alike, their identities interchangeable, and their struggles equivalent. A famous example of cultural homogenization occurred in Coca-Cola's widely seen advertisement in the 1970s in which children represented cultures from around the world, singing together and, of course, drinking Coke. To many critics, the ad symbolized the tendency of globalization to discount or caricature cultural difference while reducing individuals to the status of potential consumers. Underlying the ad's overt message of representing global harmony via a song, the message of homogenization conveyed by the ad was that a specific kind of consumerism—the purchase and consumption of Coca-Cola—was what provided a sense of global unity and harmony. As George Richardson pointed out in this context,

> Cultural homogenization reduces existing cultures to superficial parodies of themselves and in suggesting that these pale imitations are the essences of local cultures, it minimizes significant differences that can and do exist between cultural groups. Ultimately, cultural homogenization is a form of cultural repression rather than an open expression of cultural difference.

Particularly in television advertisements, cultural homogenization has become so pervasive that many students have ceased to
remark on its underlying message of consumerism and cultural
conformity.[19]

Coke isn't the only company to promote global cultural homogenization. In China, Latin America, the Pacific Rim, South America,
Africa, and the industrialized world, adults and young people alike
want Nike sneakers, Gap clothes, Hollywood blockbuster movies,
the latest television programs and mass-market books. Around the
world, corporate culture from the industrialized world is coming
into contact with local tradition, knowledge, skills, artisans, and
values. At the same time, the rapid increase of cultural migration
from the developing nations is having its own effect on the world
as populations shift and new cultures are integrated into those
of dominant nations. Rarely today is a community composed of
people with identical backgrounds. These new mixtures of people
and cultures call for continued attentiveness when engaging people
deemed "different" or "foreign" to a given culture.

Unstable Meanings

Social relationships do not exist in a vacuum. The ways we relate
to one another are informed by our identities, the languages we
use to communicate, and our perceptions of interpersonal power.
Identity is informed by both difference and sameness. It is what sets
us apart from others and gives us a sense of self. At the same time,
identity binds us to other people by making us feel we are members of a collectivity. The psychological idea of identity is related
to a person's view or mental model of him or herself. The term

"identity" refers to the capacity for self-reflection and the awareness of self. In sociology and political science, the notion of identity has more to do with the ways people see themselves as members of groups—determined by such factors as social class, subculture, or ethnicity. This is the sense in which political scientists speak of national identity and feminists speak of gender identity.

Because so much of our identity is determined by the world around us, it is common for people to think of identity as fixed or given. Individuals understand that they are born as men or women—and that is the end of the story. Contemporary theorists of identity have taken issue with notions of stable and unchanging identities—recognizing that people can alter their identities or present themselves to others in different ways. Judith Butler asserts that people perform their identities, especially when it comes to gender. Butler has written that "what we take to be an internal essence of gender is manufactured through a sustained set of acts, posited through the gendered stylization of the body."[20] Butler asserts that "what we take to be an 'internal' feature of ourselves is one that "we anticipate and produce through certain bodily acts, at an extreme, an hallucinatory effect of naturalized gestures."[21]

Butler's view of identity as unfixed and mutable is informed by principles of postmodern theory. Postmodernism asserts that the traditional ideas and practices of modernism—manifest in such things as art, architecture, literature, religious faith, and scientific knowledge—have become outdated in the face of new economic, social, and political realities. As such, conventional rules could be questioned at home, school, and the workplace. Language received a great deal of attention from postmodern scholars because it so affects what people know and believe. Some theorists challenged conventional methods of reading and writing, asserting, for example, that readers no longer needed to satisfy themselves with books as written. Michel Foucault wrote that the "frontiers of a book are never clear-cut" because "it is caught up in a system of references to other books, other texts, other sentences: it is a node within a network."[22] This relationship to other written works allows the reader to become more than a partner in the creation of meaning; it begins to throw into question the category of authorship itself. In this way the presumed authority of authors is revealed, along with the institutional frameworks holding it in place. As Foucault explains,

> The "author-function" is tied to the legal and institutional systems that circumscribe, determine, and articulate the realm of discourses; it does not operate in a uniform manner in all discourses, at all times, and in any given culture it is not defined by the spontaneous attribution of a text to its creator, but through a series of precise and complex procures; it does not refer, purely and simply, to an actual individual.[23]

This suggests some intriguing political possibilities. By casting doubt on such categories as copyright and originality, the very premise of literary authority becomes undermined. Subverted by extension are the hierarchies of knowledge that support such institutions.

In literary and film studies in the early 1990s, similar ideas of empowered readership became popular in academic circles. Theories were advanced which touted the native abilities of audiences to contest intended meanings of films and television programs—or to make up new interpretations of their own. With added education, it was argued, viewers could further gird themselves against the manipulations of advertisers while also developing richer means of enjoying entertainment. The flaw in this discourse lay in the absence of any empirical grounding, for little scholarship could document the political claims of its proponents.[24] Rather than illustrating any substantive activism, such work would often dwell on the resistant activities of *Desperate Housewives* or *Lost* viewers, who would use existing texts as points of departure for personal fantasy. Worse still, like much unchannelled rebellion, this behavior was often less than enlightened in its orientation. It would as frequently replicate popular stereotypes of race, class, and gender as it would challenge them. This point is conceded by fan-club analyst Henry Jenkins, who states that "readers are not always resistant; all resistant readings are not necessarily progressive readings; the 'people' do not always recognize their conditions of alienation and subordination."[25]

These postmodern principles of shifting identities and destabilized authority lead to some uncomfortable conculsions. If people perceive themselves as free from tradition and control, they take on a great deal more responsibility for their actions. This is where critical education comes in. Without critical skills people are vulnerable to the vagaries of persuasion and subjectivity that they encounter continually in daily life. How else does one gird oneself from the manipulations of desire and fear?

Fear, Ethics, and Everyday Life

Fear is a part of everyday life—and it motivates much of what we do. It is not simply a fear of immediate danger, but also a broader fear that we're doing something wrong or that we aren't all that we should be or could be. These feelings are no accident. They are not in any way a "natural" part of us. We get them from somewhere. That somewhere is the culture around us. That's why they work. On a conscious level, we are aware that our immediate surroundings, the things we consume, and broader world we inhabit are all fraught with dangers. We can minimize these dangers by knowing where hazards lurk, being smart about how we live, and protecting ourselves and our loved ones in every way we can. But safety from danger comes with a price. To feel secure we alter the way we act, make compromises in what we want to achieve, and pay—on many levels—for a perception of safety. We do what is necessary to protect our health, we buy products or services that will help us look good and successfully integrate into society. We support a legal system and legislature that will act on our behalf to protect us, using violent means—and even killing other people—if necessary. This is the true damage effected by representations of aggression, crime, and war. The true "effects" of such material create what veteran media scholar George Gerbner has called the "mean world" syndrome—the belief that our world is a dangerous place where simplistically defined forces of good and evil are continually in conflict, where movie-style heroes and villains really exist, and where violent force is necessary to sustain our ongoing well-being.[26]

This makes fear a part of everyday experience. It's more than an occasional scare from a horror movie or a phobia about germs or an airplane flight or al-Qaeda. Anxiety can affect our sense of who we are and who we might become. People experience so many fears in so many aspects of life that a feeling of fear starts to control them and their society. Much news and entertainment is driven by stories that produce fear, and many of the consumer products we buy and use are intended to ward off various insecurities and anxieties.

Where does such thinking come from? Why does such anxiety persist in the absence of verifying evidence or logical inquiry? The answer is that collective fear is a social construction driven by money and sustained by social anxiety in an era of growing uncertainty. In recent years, a number of well-researched books have discussed our skittish culture. Barry Glassner's *The Culture of Fear: Why Americans Are Afraid of the Wrong Things* largely criticizes hyperbolic news and entertainment media for frightening people.[27] David L. Altheide's *Creating Fear: News and the Construction of Crisis* discusses what he terms "the problem frame" that "promotes a discourse of fear that may be defined as the pervasive communication, symbolic awareness, and expectation that danger and risk are a central feature of the effective environment."[28] Wole Soyinkkas's *The Climate of Fear: The Quest for Dignity in a Dehumanized World* says the anxieties once focused on nuclear annihilation now have attach themselves to other ideas, especially in the post–9/11 years.[29] Corey Robin's *Fear: The History of a Political Idea* addresses concerns about international conflict and potential attacks on civilian populations. Robin also looks at the increases in public anxiety since September 11, 2001.[30]

It's important to stress that despite the cloud of confusion in the public generated by post–9/11 media, broad social anxieties were well in place before those tragedies. In 1999, Zygmunt Bauman eloquently wrote of the growing mood of "uncertainty, insecurity, and unsafety" in contemporary society.[31] Increasingly people feel abandoned by public institutions and deceived by corporations. The majority hate their leaders yet never vote. Some would call this a postmodern movement in which the monolithic certainties of a prior era have been thrown into question. Widespread public insecurity has opened the door to a new form of authoritarianism that promises protection. Anxieties produced by a rapidly changing world are soothed by media narratives of a fantasized return to origins.

Think about all of the disappointments and reasons people have to be worried about once-stable public symbols. From America's failure in Vietnam to the nation's shame over Nixon's resignation to the Reagan administration's Iran-Contra problem to the exploits of Bill Clinton—people have had good reason to lose faith in the presidency. Religion hasn't fared much better, with sex scandals in the Catholic Church and the hysteria of U.S. religious hardliners. Corporate misbehavior and greed reached such proportions that Congress, after much arm twisting, passed the Sarbanes/Oxley Act to throw CEOs in jail. Celebrities haven't fared well either. Consider Martha Stewart, Rush Limbaugh, William Bennett, Michael Jackson, and a host of other less pious public figures who fell for vices ranging from drug abuse to child molestation. Of course, the favorite targets have always been African American men. Think of O. J. Simpson, Kobe Bryant, and Michael Jackson—guilty or innocent—put up for public pillory. It's been a sad era for role models.

Then there is the economy. The long-term outlook isn't good. Average Americans don't need to be told that their money is buying less, good jobs are harder to find, and that much of what they put on their backs, drive, and listen to is made in the growing economic powerhouse that is Asia. As the gap between rich and poor continues to widen in Western nations, countries in Africa and parts of Asia and Latin America fall further into misery and despair. And it isn't someone else's problem when billions of people are hungry and diseased because extremist factions in these nations are growing increasingly angry about the global imbalance in power and resources. Although the United States and its allies may say that they don't believe it, desperate people around the world hoping for a day of reckoning are finding common cause in their hatred of nations that callously exploit the rest of the world. After all, that was the real message delivered by the bombings in New York, London, Spain, and scores of lesser-known locations throughout Iraq, Afghanistan, and other nations. People in industrialized nations have every reason to be nervous that the intensity of such attacks will only increase as their governments continue to ignore the reasons why they occur.

Crime and Daily Routines

Representations of crime and war face us every day in different forms. Drama and news programs provide endlessly repeated narratives of threats or assaults. This programming helps convince citizens of the need for even stronger police protection and more draconian laws to punish offenders. Once the leading nation in the production and distribution of entertainment, the United States remains the world leader in the commission of state-sanctioned aggression.[32] The United States is the only Western nation to use the death penalty; 73.4 percent of its citizens support the policy.[33] As rates of crime have gradually decreased during the past decade, prison construction has become the nation's fastest growing industry.[34] Of the two million people incarcerated in the United States, half are African American and seventy percent are illiterate.[35] Is it merely coincidence that the majority of criminals depicted in movies and television programs are people of color?

Obviously, the mass media do not create these circumstances. But constant exposure to stories of violent crime create an environment of suggestibility. In the 1930s, Walter Lippman wrote in his classic book *Public Opinion* that people cannot gather from direct experience the information they need to function as citizens in a democratic society. They rely on various kinds of media to form their opinions. Today, seventy-six percent of Americans say that they base their perceptions about crime on what they see on TV and read in the newspaper.[36] This leads to regrettable misconceptions. The coverage of crime in the news does not correspond with the occurrence of crime in society. As Lori Dorfman and Vincent Schiraldi write:

> Violent crime dominates crime coverage. Crime is often the
> dominant topic on local television news, network news, and

TV news magazines. In general, TV crime reporting is the
inverse of crime frequency. That is, murder is reported most
often on news though it happens the least. Several analyses of
evening news found that, although homicides made up from
two-tenths of one percent of all arrests, homicides made up
more than a quarter (25–27 percent) of crimes reported on
the news.[37]

Even as crime rates have decreased, coverage of crime has increased.
Between 1990 and 1998, national crime rates fell by 20 percent, as
network television showed an 83 percent increase in crime news.[38]
Homicide coverage rose by 473 percent as homicides declined by
33 percent.[39]

The reasons for these disparities between fact and fiction are
economic in part. As television networks and movie studios become subsidiaries of multinational conglomerates, pressure has
grown to deliver profits. News programs compete with each other
and with entertainment programs for viewers. As a consequence
they become splashier and more oriented toward the spectacular.
The effects of this sensationalism are hardly neutral. They create
an atmosphere that enabled California's passage in 1994 of voter
initiative Proposition 184, the nation's first "Three Strikes" law.
The law was established shortly after the widely publicized abduc-
tion and murder of eight-year-old Polly Klaas and the crusade-like
media campaign for the law led by the child's father. In the summer
of 2002, the powerful effect of stories about victimized children
led to the implementation of a system of statewide media alerts
reminiscent of air raid warnings. This occurred despite a decline
in child abductions.

Without a doubt, the culture of fear that results from the mis-
representation of threats to the public creates an ugly situation.
But it does something more. It sets up a tempting opportunity

for politicians eager to please voters or to get government to take certain actions. Someone running for office can get the support of anxious voters by promising to hire more police or make the army stronger. For this kind of election campaign it's helpful in a cynical kind of way for people to be frightened or if they think they are in danger. People running for office throughout the history of the United States and other nations have used public worries about crime, or immigration, or threats from other countries to convince voters that they were the right candidates for the jobs. As you might expect, it's been an effective strategy and one that's a lot easier to use than making a case for getting elected on issues like the environment or jobs. The 2007 murder of thirty-two people by a Virginia Tech student capped a decade of more than thirty well-publicized school shootings in the United States and abroad, which have resulted in broad-based changes in school security policies, renewed calls for gun control, and enhanced legislation aimed at preventing similar incidents. Some experts have described anxieties about school shootings as a new type of moral panic in the United States and other nations.

The practice of using threats to manipulate politics has been in the news quite a bit in the recent decade, especially in the United States. In domestic politics it came up during the 1980s and 1990s in California and in certain states along the Mexican border when a number of politicians began to blame rising rates of unemployment, welfare dependency, and educational failure on illegal immigrants entering the United States from the south. Throughout 2006, the U.S. Congress and President Bush argued for months over the nation's use of illegal Mexican immigrants. This led to tighter border controls and the passage of harsh laws to punish undocumented workers discovered in America—even though the economies of those states heavily depended on the willingness of the illegals to do difficult work for low wages. Eventually, it became evident that the economic and social problems were not caused by immigrants and many of the laws were repealed.

This propagation of misinformation has even more profound effects for foreign policy and defense. These are areas considerably more removed from people's lived experience than crime and hence even more contingent on media representation. On some issues, the federal government now literally writes the news. A secondary effect of the monetary squeeze on network news departments has been the virtual elimination of investigatory journalism. Although much was made of governmental media manipulation during the 1992 Desert Storm offensive, television had for some years already capitulated to the Pentagon and White House information offices in its near total reliance on them for government-related content. Regardless of one's opinion about the war on terrorism, there is little doubt that public knowledge about the campaign is limited to what Washington releases. This is done because war is the ultimate example of rationalized state aggression. To gain public consent for war its stakes must be raised to the level of myth and history.

In the discourse of media fear, no figure of otherness surpasses that of the terrorist. Writing in 1999, Elayne Rapping argued that "terrorists are portrayed as irrational, inscrutable, and inherently violent. They threaten to infiltrate our porous border, bringing with them fear, chaos, and disorder."[40] This creates the impression that terrorists can't be rehabilitated because they cannot be reconciled with our system of logic and justice. Framing terrorists in this way encourages the establishment of more powerful methods of law enforcement and incarceration because terrorists cannot recognize or comprehend standard means. To Rapping, "terrorists are marked in the media by dramatic signs of difference, physical and psychological. These signs are so repellant and horrifying that they easily justify the use of measures previously unthinkable in the enforcement of 'normal' criminal law because terrorists are not 'normal' criminals; they are alien, inhuman monsters."[41]

These remarks remind us that the reactions of the Bush administration, regarded by some as cynically theatrical and politically opportunistic, have deeper roots in past events. But network news rarely provides much depth or historical perspective. Connections rarely are made between the prior three decades of terrorist assaults on U.S. holdings—not to mention the sponsorship or direct execution of terrorism by the United States in Afghanistan, Angola, China, Indonesia, Lebanon, Russia, Sudan, Syria, Turkey, and Vietnam. The difference is that recent assaults have been on American soil—and that was exactly their point.

Notes

1. Lucy Lippard, *Mixed Blessings: New Art in a Multicultural America* (New York: Pantheon, 1990), 19.

2. Lippart, 49.

3. Phyllis Raybin Emert, "Native American Mascots: Racial Slur or Cherished Tradition?" New Jersey State Bar Foundation, Winter 2003. *http://www.njsbf.com/njsbf/student/respect/winter03-1.cfm*. Accessed May 20, 2006.

4. Ibid.

5. Lippard, 33.

6. Michael Eric Dyson, *Holler if You Hear Me: Searching for Tupac Shakur* (New York: Basic Civitas Books, 2001), 50.

7. bell hooks, *Black Looks: Race and Representation* (Boston: South End Press, 1992), 35–36.

8. Peter McLaren, *Revolutionary Multiculturalism: Pedagogies of Dissent for the New Millennium* (Boulder, Co: Westview Press, 1997), 154.

9. Hector St. John de Crevecoeur, *Letters From An American Farmer* (New York: Kessinger Publishing, 2004), 22.

10. Michael Sokolove, "The Believer," *New York Times Magazine* *http://www.nytimes.com,* May 22, 2005. Internet reference. Accessed July 16, 2007.

11. "Bush urges gay marriage ban enshrined in Constitution," *http://.www.CNN.com,* June 3, 2006. Accessed June 15, 2006.

12. Ibid.

13. Howard Becker, *Outsiders: Studies in the Sociology of Deviance* (New York: Free Press, 1997).

14. Julius Debro, "Dialogue with Howard S. Becker (1970)," in Howard S. Becker, *Doing Things Together: Selected Papers* (Chicago: Northwestern University Press, 1986), 33.

15. Normative behavior is a term used in sociology to describe actions intended to normalize something or make it acceptable.

16. Gregory Jay, *What Is Multiculturalism?*, Dec. 2002. *http://www. uwm.edu/~gjay/Multicult/Multiculturalism.html.* Accessed Sept. 11, 2006.

17. Ibid.

18. Molefi Kete Asante, *The Afrocentric Idea* (Philadelphia: Temple University, 1998).

19. George Richardson, "Two Terms You Can (and Should) Use in the Classroom: Cultural Homogenization and Eurocentrism." *http://www. quasar.ualberta.ca/css/CSS_35_1/two_terms_you_can_use.htm.* Accessed Dec. 19, 2006.

20. Judith Butler, *Gender Trouble: Feminism and the Subversion of Identity* (New York and London: Routledge, 1990), xvi.

21. Ibid.

22. Michel Foucault, *The Archaeology of Knowledge,* trans. A. M. Sheridan Smith (New York: Harper Colophon, 1976), 23.

23. Foucault as cited in George Landow, *Hypertext: The Conversion of Technology and Contemporary Critical Theory* (Baltimore: Johns Hopkins University Press, 1991), 91.

24. Constance Penley and Andrew Ross, eds., *Technoculture*

(Minneapolis: University of Minnesota, 1991); Henry Jenkins, *Textual Poachers: Television Fans and Participatory Culture* (New York and London: Routledge, 1992); Allucquére Rosanne Stone, *The War of Desire and Technology at the Close of the Mechanical Age* (Cambridge: MIT Press, 1996).

25. Jenkins, 34.

26. George Gerbner, "Reclaiming Our Cultural Mythology," *The Ecology of Justice*, 38 (Spring 1994), 40.

27. Barry Glassner, *The Culture of Fear: Why Americans Are Afraid of the Wrong Things* (New York: Basic Books, 1999).

28. David L. Altheide, *Creating Fear: News and the Construction of Crisis*, (New York: Walter de Gruyter, 2002).

29. Wole Soyinkkas, *The Climate of Fear: The Quest for Dignity in a Dehumanized World* (New York: Random House, 2004).

30. Corey Robin, *Fear: The History of a Political Idea* (Cambridge: Oxford University Press, 2004).

31. Zygmunt Bauman, *In Search of Politics* (Stanford: Stanford University Press, 1999), 5.

32. Hugo Adam Bedau and Paul G. Cassell. *Debating the Death Penalty: Should America Have Capital Punishment?* (Cambridge: Oxford University Press, 2004).

33. Ibid.

34. Ibid.

35. Ibid.

36. Lori Dorfman and Vincent Schiraldi, Building Blocks for Youth, "Off Balance: Youth, Race, and Crime in the News." *http://buildingblocksforyouth.org*. Accessed July 10, 2006.

37. Ibid.

38. Ibid.

39. Ibid.

40. Rapping, "Aliens, Nomads, Mad Dogs," 268.

41. Ibid.

CHAPTER FIVE

JOINING

COMMUNITIES AND PUBLICS

Joining is a critical aspect of everyday culture. Beyond the atomized observations and actions we take as individuals lie the myriad manifestations of our lives in relationship to others. We define ourselves in relationship to a world of experiences and things, but more importantly, to a world of other people, our interactions with them, and their understanding of us. This chapter looks at groups, collective understandings, institutions, and life in the public realm. It examines the roles that audiences play in making things famous, responding to marketing campaigns, or taking part in elections. Also addressed is the fundamental way that many of our social interactions constitute a form of ongoing education. We are continually in a process of learning from each other and teaching, whether we realize it or not. The importance of these educational processes and their relationship to everyday life are addressed in the field of "critical pedagogy," which has attracted interest in recent decades as an extension of cultural studies. Critical pedagogy asserts that education takes place in many places besides schools and at different times in our lives, and that these educational encounters are structured into many of the institutions and relationships we take for granted. For this reason a comprehensive consideration of the everyday calls for an examination of its pedagogical dimensions.

Also addressed in this section are the ways that our daily experiences lead to the formation of opinions and perspectives on public life. Social interactions and exposure to mass media inevitably lead to agreement or disagreement with public policy, ethical positions, group behavior, or even governmental actions. But do our opinions follow prescribed patterns or fall into generalized categories? If the "self" that many people believe belongs only to them is as constructed as linguists and social scientists tell us, perhaps our opinions are not entirely our own either. With this in mind, discussion here then turns to the ways that public communication is controlled either by direct manipulation or by market forces. How can anything as coercive as censorship exist at a time when many people believe the flow of information is unmediated and we live in a "free society"?

The first essay in this chapter, "Dialogue and Voice," examines basic issues in communication within groups based on principles of critical pedagogy. Developed initially by Brazilian expatriate Paulo Freire, critical pedagogy stresses the importance of dialogue between people and the crucial need for individuals to develop analytical capabilities in addressing collective problems. Building on these issues of dialogue and public communication, the essay "Public Opinion" considers the kinds of ideas and arguments that then get communicated. Opinions do not simply occur in a vacuum but have philosophical backgrounds that often can be traced to "idealist" and "realist" traditions of thought. Finally, the essay "Free Speech and Censorship" examines what happens to ideas as they seek to find expression. Do ideas travel unproblematically from speaker to listener, or do they encounter regulation, control, or outright interference?

Dialogue and Voice

Language and literacy are important themes in joining because they play such major roles in the way we interact with the world and respond to it. As discussed in Chapter 3, written literacy is essential to such basic activities as applying for a driver's license or completing a job application. Most uses of the term literacy are specific to a given language and are limited by which language is being used. The choice of language determines who is literate. It controls who can function effectively in a society. Because it can grant or deny access to social mobility—and even survival in some instances—language carries with it enormous economic and political power.

Author and educator bell hooks has written extensively about literacy and its relationship to social status. To hooks, literacy can have a broader meaning beyond the simple ability to read and write. After all, the basic skills of literacy do not in themselves guarantee anything. The key is how literacy is used. Hooks uses two concepts to discuss this issue: *critical literacy* and *agency*. An individual exhibits critical literacy when the tools of reading and writing are actively applied to examining and questioning texts. Critical literacy entails looking below the surface of messages, speakers, and institutions (i.e., government and the media) from which they emerge. Critical literacy skills reside in all people, but they are not always used. This is another way that the emancipatory capacities of everyday culture need to be nurtured and cultivated to become effective. Hooks believes that education can play a pivotal role in bringing critical literacy to life in people. Agency might be described as the decision to act upon critical literacy. If people are mentally questioning messages, the next step might be to do something with the answers. One way hooks suggests that agency operates is when people "talk back," that is, comment upon, support, or criticize what they see.

Many of hooks's teachings emerged from her own experiences. She writes that, growing up, she wasn't always encouraged to speak and express her opinions. Like many young people, hooks says that she was made to feel that her views didn't matter and that articulating them wouldn't make much of a difference. Inspired by a favorite grandmother, hooks eventually found the ability to talk back in a process she terms "coming to voice." The journey of coming to voice in American society is not necessarily an easy one, hooks cautions, especially for women and people of color. Yet it is an important component to the agency that people need for their emotional well-being and that society needs for the democratic exchange of ideas and opinions. Central in much of hooks's work are the premises of critical pedagogy.

Critical pedagogy is an amalgam of radical philosophies that first gained wide recognition in the 1970s through the writings of Freire.[1] As practiced by Freire in countries throughout the third world, the doctrines of critical pedagogy were used by colonized citizens to analyze their roles in relations of oppression and to devise programs for revolutionary change. To Freire, this analytical process grew directly from an everyday process of dialogue among disempowered people, rather than from the top-down dictates of an intellectual vanguard. The notion of dialogue was the ideal antidote for citizens who had always been told what to do by oppressive leaders. Rather than subordinate "objects" in a one-directional address from dominant figures, participants in a dialogue become "subjects" who can jointly share ideas.

The political implications of this philosophy derive from its related emphasis on praxis—the linkage of theory to action. As Freire puts it, "a revolution is achieved with neither verbalism nor activism, but rather with praxis, that is, with reflection and action directed at the structures to be transformed. The revolutionary effort to transform these structures radically cannot designate its leaders as its *thinkers* and the oppressed as mere *doers*."[2] Freire and his colleagues aggressively advocated the extrapolation of this program for revolutionary action into a range of social contexts and political institutions. In this way the concept of critical pedagogy became synonymous with a variety of interventions both inside and outside the classroom. During the 1970s and 1980s, the philosophies of critical pedagogy were adapted throughout the industrialized world as a means of addressing power imbalances there. Significant in this regard are the scholarly writings of Michael Apple, Antonia Darder, Henry Giroux, Joe E. Kinchloe, Peter McLaren, and Rodolfo Torres.

Critical pedagogy also addresses the hierarchies of power inherent in educational relationships. Rather than reinforcing conventional top-down teacher/student relationships, critical pedagogy acknowledges student voice as well as youthful resistance to authority. Critical pedagogy offers strategies for redirecting resistant impulses in positive ways. Rather than simply accepting lessons as given, students are encouraged to bring their own insights to the pedagogical encounter. No longer do texts need to be interpreted as intended by their authors or manufacturers. Texts can be revised, combined, or contested according to the reader's interpretive capabilities. This leads to broadened considerations of the many issues that contextualize culture and education. Factors such as personal history and group identity begin to be examined in relation to language, technology, and power. Moreover, this expanded view of education challenged strictly aesthetic definitions of culture by reading into the very fabric of all political and social relations. Because culture and experience are subject to multiple readings, meaning became a matter of contest in the broadest possible terms.

Much of the movement's vocabulary of "empowerment," "dialogue," and "voice" has entered the lexicon of Western social reform movements. At the same time, the principles of critical pedagogy have undergone significant modifications that adapt them to the needs of contemporary technocratic societies. In a world that is rapidly redefining relations between its centers and margins and questioning the legitimacy of master narratives, critical pedagogy's analytical strategies have been modified with theories of postmodernism, feminism, gay and lesbian studies, postcolonial theory, and youth culture. In different ways, each of these discourses has advanced the concepts of critical pedagogy by challenging it to be more self-reflexive and attentive to its own internal biases, hierarchies, and solipsisms.

Pedagogy outside the Classroom

The development of critical pedagogy, media literacy, and other philosophies of radical education owes a great deal to the writings of Antonio Gramsci. Concerned with finding practical applications for Marxist theories, Gramsci saw social change as a process of learning in which ordinary people come to formulate a new social order. Gramsci stressed the importance of what he termed "creative" knowledge in which "learning takes place especially through a spontaneous and continuous effort of the pupil, with the teacher only exercising a function of a friendly guide."[3] Like Freire, Gramsci believed that principles of revolution would emerge from the oppressed. For Gramsci, every relationship of hegemony is necessarily an educational relationship. In this context he was referring not simply to the forms of teaching that one commonly associates with the classroom. Gramsci was describing the profoundly political process through which citizens are socialized to recognize and validate state power. This process infuses all components of the social apparatus: the office, the church, the museum, and particularly the school. If we think of these institutions as sites of potential ideological persuasion, then Gramsci's theory of education becomes significant. Obviously we are nearly always in a process of learning.

This form of radical pedagogy has great significance as a democratizing practice. In contrast to the conservative impulse to remove ever-larger regions of experience from public discussion, a Gramscian pedagogy recognizes the implications of everyday events. This means admitting that many areas that claim neutrality in our lives are in fact sites of profound ideological struggle. Television newscasts, school curricula, computer programs, scientific breakthroughs, "great" works of literature—these are not objective phenomena that somehow exist outside the realm of ideology. They are forms of representation invested with specific interests in every manifestation. Through these texts dominance strives to replicate itself, often disguising its actions in the process. This invisibility of the center is often accompanied by a quiet exclusion of otherness. People may be concerned about the violent suppression of certain dissenting voices, yet at the same time they may be unaware of those silently consigned to the structured absences of discourse. In this sense, every act of writing, of film production, of curriculum design, of institutional organization is an act of inclusion and exclusion. Therefore, these and other social forms must be continually scrutinized for what they represent.

Recognition of educational potentials outside the classroom has led many teachers to rethink their roles. This same impulse has also helped others in such noneducational sites as arts organizations, neighborhood centers, recreational facilities, hospitals, theaters, and jails to reconfigure their programs along more pedagogical lines. This type of institutional border crossing has been encouraged by interdisciplinary academic areas like ethnic studies, media studies, and cultural studies. Equally significant has been the broad-based recognition that conventional methods for reaching students, clients, or audiences are no longer adequate. New methods and structures are needed that can combine scarce resources and forms of expertise in ways that overcome rigid protocols and conventional institutional designs.

The emphasis of radical educators on participation and dialogue has encouraged many to focus on issues of critical literacy as an important democratizing tool. Not only can interpretive strategies assist viewers in understanding potentially manipulative media messages, these tools can also enhance the pleasure of consuming media. By affording audiences a role in the communicative transaction, one does not deny the overwhelming influences public media command. Instead, this suggests that viewers and consumers of culture have a stake in the process that can be enhanced through education.

Reasonable as it seems, these premises of critical literacy run counter to the commonsense thinking of many parents, politicians, and educators. Arguments generally fall into two equally deficient categories: the first negatively asserts that popular culture deceives and degrades the thinking of viewers; the second claims that media innocently reflect the actual wants and needs of audiences. The difficult idea for some is that both assertions may be true simultaneously. Communications technologies are as much *descriptive* as they are *prescriptive,* existing in a dialectical relationship with lived experience. Each informs and is informed by the other.

Beyond this, the study of popular culture holds importance as a means of validating the relevance of different vocabularies, canons, aesthetic registers, discursive forms, and sites of cultural articulation. A democratic society is enhanced by pedagogies that encourage the production of diverse identities and knowledge forms, rather than restricting such possibilities. Answering these questions involves finding the means to question ways we read and interpret everyday experience. It means revealing the ways received meanings are bound in specific histories and modes of address (or use) that act as limits to human possibility. This leads to a recognition of the creative development of meanings and interpretations. It evolves from the understanding of the mediated character of all representation and consequent ability of people to invent new or alternate readings. Such activity might range from benign arguments following a film over what it really meant to the elaborate fantasy rituals, social events, and even conventions attached to such television programs as *American Idol* or *Lost*.

This more active posture of reception implies that viewers, users, or purchasers of texts and objects need not accept the roles they have been assigned by an author or manufacturer. Audiences possess the capacity to exceed their purportedly passive roles, to subvert given identities, or create new visions of themselves. Ultimately this can be a point of initiation for citizens to develop their own stories, or dream their own dreams. No better example of this exists than the practice in rap and hip-hop composition of "sampling"—a process enabled by relatively inexpensive recording technology. Sampling entails the often repeated use of a segment from one recording to another. In this act of appropriation the original piece is both used and changed by virtue of its new context. The individual sampling is at once a listener and a creator of the music.

These productive capacities entail a critical engagement with market forces. In this sense people need to recognize both the extent and limits of choice in the selection of narratives and consumer goods. Obviously, one is always constrained by the range of stories, ingredients, and commodities that are available and affordable. Yet at the same time, within these parameters options with tactical applications exist. As Lisa Tiersten argues, it is time to move beyond the simple consumer-as-victim mentalities that characterized much early writing on advertising.[4] Such negative discourses range from self-limiting suggestions of false consciousness to psychological claims of subliminal seduction. What needs to be stressed instead is the degree to which audiences are not always fooled by the media. People *do* exercise agency in the acquisition and use of products; consumer advocacy groups and product boycotts *have* had an impact on what gets shown on television and what ends up on store shelves. The corporate production of texts and objects does not exert a total authority over buyers, but functions in a relationship of exchange.

These critical understandings enhance democracy in expanding people's ability to choose, not merely from an array of preselected goods, but from among options to reject, alter, or creatively use what they view or buy. Since reception and use are active gestures, educators need to recognize that the potential for productive culture inheres in the very fabric of life. Like talking, it lives in the ways people communicate to each other, in the objects they make, and the stories they tell. It permeates the rituals of meeting, listening, dancing, joke telling, playing sports, and making pictures. Most importantly, it inheres in the ways that people make choices, invent their lives, and adapt to difficult circumstances. In this latter sense, culture is, as Paul Willis has stated, the very stuff of survival.[5] Such a broadened definition of education constitutes a means of encouraging people to assert more control over their lives. This pedagogy suggests that choices exist where none were seen and creativity is possible where none was expected. In this renewed source of agency the promise of democracy can be rekindled.

Public Opinion

How do opinions take form in everyday life? What is the relationship between belief and argument? Reason and rhetoric?

Take apart any argument and you'll find a disagreement over values, such as those found in the opposition of idealist versus realist philosophies. Idealist thinking has its roots in the Western enlightenment and the premises of modernism associated with it. Many debates in contemporary society have their roots in the fundamental clash between idealism (which tends to correspond to conservative attitudes toward government regulation and social policy) and realism (which is often identified with aspects of liberal approaches to governance and social reform). Idealism, which should not be confused with the popular notion of an idealistic or virtuous individual, supports a belief in broad, abstract values that guide people and take precedence over immediate concerns. For this reason idealism tends to place less value on everyday experience and concerns. Realism privileges concrete circumstances and argues that larger principles should be derived from recognizable needs. Realism regards the everyday as the starting point for philosophy, social analysis, and public policy.

Idealism

Idealism refers to the opinion that reality can only be described from some point of view, not in a way that transcends all points of view. Idealism holds that reality is mind-correlative or mind-coordinated. To idealists, tangible objects are not independent of the conscious mind, but exist only through processes of intellectual operations. The everyday world of things and people is not the real world but a representation as it appears to be. Late eighteenth-century philosopher George W. F. Hegel argued that an internal spirit guides all perceptions, including human reason. Hegel described a "world soul," existing through all history, which emerges from a process now known as the Hegelian dialectic. A contemporary of Hegel, Immanuel Kant wrote that the mind shapes our perceptions of the world to take form in both time and space. Kant believed that all we can know are mental impressions of an outside world. Such mental impressions may or may not exist independently from the real because we can never access that outside world directly.

Idealists view people as governed by universal truths to which they should always aspire but can never achieve. These transcendental values exist for all time and apply to all people, regardless of their historical circumstance or cultural heritage. In social terms, idealists tend to put their emphasis on behavior, attributing human success or failure to attitudes people bring to their exercise of free agency. Thus values like paternal authority and marriage are held up as goals to which everyone should subscribe. Idealists see a fundamental correctness in existing arrangements, but fear its enabling values are eroding. This logic argues that job discrimination, sexual harassment, and unfair housing practices really aren't that much of a problem, and the government programs to rectify them provide inegalitarian preferences upon which minority groups become dependent. Great importance is afforded to cultural issues, as manifest in recent controversies over literary canons, artistic censorship, and the labeling of records and video games. Culture is seen as the embodiment of these timeless values, not the reflection of everyday life or work. Idealist culture manifests itself in a chosen list of great books and masterpiece artworks housed in special preserves of aesthetic contemplation. Separated from the exigencies of daily life, art is seen as devoid of political content or implication. Ironically, rarely is any consideration given to the corrupting influence of a market that emphasizes competition, greed, and wealth as measures of human worth.

Realism

Realism assumes that reality inheres in everyday experience and that its functions can be accessed and known. Because what we know derives from the here and now, realism relies on descriptions of objects and environments. Realism recognizes the importance of ordinary observations and events. It tends to reject idealistic views of the heroic and transcendental. In the early 1600s, realist philosopher René Descartes asserted that knowledge derives from the senses and that we understand abstractions by relating them to our actual experiences of the world. Writing in the latter half of the seventeenth century, John Locke likewise asserted that there exists a perceivable world "out there" that has certain qualities that underly our broader understandings and knowledge.

Realists see truth emerging from the lived experiences of human beings. Such realists recognize that values develop differently from culture to culture and from era to era. Rules about gender relationships or family structures are not permanently fixed but need to be evaluated in the context of changing social needs. Realists are often critical of a society they believe is emphasizing greed and competition rather than social justice. As a consequence, realists promote government programs to correct the inequities produced by market forces. Rather than attempting to manipulate people into adopting social norms, realists seek ways of broadening society to be more inclusive—more tolerant of diversity and difference. Instead of blaming people in need for their circumstances, realists are more likely to favor a fundamental redistribution of wealth through such measures as welfare programs, government subsidies, and progressive tax legislation. Arguments that some people might lack motivation or require forms of moral education are rejected as biased. This fundamentally redistributive program has made realists (who generally ascribe to liberal social policies) vulnerable to the charge that they simply want to throw resources at problems. As journalist Molly Ivins jokingly stated, "This may sound simple, but the *real* problem with poor people is that they don't have enough money."[6] Because culture and art are manifestations of the daily encounters people have with one another, they can be used to educate citizens and improve their living conditions. Thus, to realists, culture is found in many places from the gallery to the classroom to the street. Because it is tied to daily life, culture always bears political implications.

In their postures of mutual exclusion, both idealist and realist camps hold part, but not all, of the means to address social problems. The inadequacy of such polarized thinking became apparent in the 1990s, with the collapse of the Eastern bloc, the election of moderate Democrat Bill Clinton, and the advent of what some termed the new "gray times." The post-2000 Bush years have signaled a return to black-and-white reasoning. Yet as the 2006 midterm elections demonstrated, Bush's failure to acknowledge a more nuanced vision is increasingly out of step with the voting public. Approaches to politics that would separate issues into neat categories—the separation of economic structure from cultural behavior—no longer seem viable. One is reminded of the words of Cornel West:

> We must acknowledge that structure and behavior are inseparable, that institutions and values go hand in hand. How people act and live are shaped—though in no way dictated or determined—by larger circumstances in which they find themselves. These circumstances can be changed, their limits attenuated, by positive actions to elevate living conditions.... We should reject the idea that structures are primarily economic and political creatures—an idea that sees culture as an ephemeral set of behavioral attitudes and values. Culture is as much a structure as the economy or politics; it is rooted in institutions such as families,

schools, churches, synagogues, mosques, and communication
industries (television, radio, video, music).[7]

As recent political contests have demonstrated, these cultural
answers to material questions hold enormous public appeal. Exit
polls indicate that the majority of voters have been motivated
more by values than any other interest. In response, the rhetoric
of both Democrats and Republicans is increasingly driven by a
vocabulary of cultural concern. Yet despite these changes in the
political climate, the polarized character of much political debate
remains resistant to change.

The path to reconciling these divergent views does not
require that one side prevail over the other. Inherent in the
founding doctrines of the United States was the principle of
tolerance for differences in opinion—of agreeing to disagree.
Many of the intellectual leaders of the American colonies came
to this conclusion on the basis of enlightenment philosophies
they brought with them from Europe. The colonies may have
been established by groups of divergent religious persuasions,
but when it became necessary to unite against the colonial
dominance of England, it was apparent that no one person
could prevail over the others. Hence, the most desirable course
was to accept differences of opinion. This became the basis of
U.S. religious tolerance. Nothing more powerful impelled the
movement toward the separation of church and state than the
realization that no one church could dominate this new state.
Many of the most distinguished leaders of the American revolution—Thomas Jefferson, George Washington, and Benjamin
Franklin—were powerfully influenced by continental enlightenment thinking on theses matters. The deity who underwrites the
concept of equality in the Declaration of Independence is the
egalitarian god who French philosopher Jean-Jacques Rousseau

worshipped, not the deity of the traditional churches that still supported and rationalized the maintenance of monarchies in nations throughout Europe. Franklin, Jefferson, and other leaders of the nascent United States spent considerable amounts of time in France associating with the intelligencia in French philosophical circles. After Franklin signed the Declaration of Independence in 1776, he became ambassador to the Court of Louis XVI. Rousseau's principles of natural law, inherent freedoms, and self-determination were part of the larger ethos of enlightenment thinking (though frequently colored by a bit of traditional religiosity) that has been called the civil religion of the United States. Separated geographically from most of the aristocrats against whom they were rebelling, the early colonists ironically were inspired by many larger principles they shared with their enemies.

Censorship and Free Speech

Most people don't spend much of their everyday life worrying about free speech or authoritarian interference with expression. The overt repression of intellectuals and journalists generally associated with censorship has largely disappeared in Western democracies. Besides its association with fascism and communism, such regulation of communication is extremely difficult to enforce in an age of cellular phones, desktop publishing, and junk faxes. Moreover, the continuing renewal of our free market economy requires the illusion of unmediated free choice—in both the grocery store and the voting booth. Even the forms of publicly sanctioned censorship that we permit for the maintenance of social compacts—copyright and libel laws, for instance—are never acknowledged as such.

Conservatives never use the word censorship, but prefer instead public accountability or standards of decency.

But censorship is a part of everyday culture nevertheless—and its threats to democracy in the United States are very real. Those attacks hit home in the censorship controversies of the early 1990s. Led by politicians such as William Dannemeyer, Jesse Helms, Dana Rohrabacher, and religious fundamentalist groups like the American Family Association and the Christian Coalition, a movement emerged in 1989 to expose allegedly immoral and anti-American arts projects supported by tax dollars. Despite the ultimate failure in enacting such sanctions, the battle that ensued on the floor of Congress and in the national news media exacted a heavy toll on the cultural funding apparatus. In addition to further alienating artists from the general public, critics of the National Endowment for the Arts (NEA) obtained a reallocation of twenty-five percent of the agency's money for state and local distribution, thus damaging the prospects of many progressive groups in conservative regions. The pre-eminence of the presidentially appointed chair of the endowment over artists' juries was also reaffirmed, thus casting an additional cloud over grant making.

Campaign promises to the contrary, President Bill Clinton demonstrated his propensity for supporting only uncontroversial art projects. In 1992, then-candidate Clinton promised an arts policy "free from political manipulation and firmly rooted in the First Amendment's freedom of expression guarantee."[8] Following the election, Clinton quickly grasped the need to conserve his political capital for other issues. In what Clinton officials asserted was an unintentional blunder, the administration even reinstated a justice department lawsuit to overturn free speech advances won by artists in court during the presidency of George H. W. Bush. During this period, Clinton's NEA chair—actress Jane

Alexander—performed more as a public relations figure than as an advocate of free speech.

In the 2000s, the administration of President George W. Bush has been less overt in its regulation of arts funding, allowing direct assaults on the arts to be carried out by state and local legislatures where Republican support is strong. Bush frequently consults with legislators like state representative Gerald Allen, who introduced a measure in Alabama to ban the use of state funds to purchase books or other materials that promote homosexuality. As Allen told one reporter, he does not want taxpayers' money to support "positive depictions of homosexuality as an alternative lifestyle."[9] Like many conservative lawmakers, Allen believes that traditional family values and traditional definitions of marriage are under attack. Within this logic, the new enemy is not al-Qaeda. The axis of evil is found in the culture and entertainment industries. We have an obligation to "save society from moral destruction," Allen explained. We have to prevent liberal librarians and trendy teachers from "re-engineering society's fabric in the minds of our children"[10]

Elsewhere, examples of regulated speech are gaining public notice with growing frequency. As controversies involving the Federal Communications Commission (FCC) have demonstrated, the effects of censorship do not stop with a specific act, but rather create a chain reaction of secondary repressions and resistances. Janet Jackson's SuperBowl fiasco or Howard Stern's scatological humor created their own political firestorms. But they also helped create an atmosphere of anxiety among broadcasters fearful of government reprisals, consumer boycotts, and declines in advertising revenues. The polarizing effect of these reactions has the unfortunate consequence of amplifying oppositions between contesting interests, generally to the benefit of the more powerful party.

These media indecency scandals have diverted public attention from more commonplace and insidious forms of censorship.

Consider institutional censorship (which is practiced by bosses, teachers, and curators); economic censorship (which determines what gets made and who can afford to have it); domestic censorship (which stifles communication in the home); and discriminatory censorship (which denies voice to particular groups). These dynamics favor certain people and ideas over others by determining not merely what can be said to whom, but also what kind of questions can be asked and through what structures discourse can evolve. As a result, those traditionally excluded from mainstream media—women, people of color, lesbians and gay men, or anyone with an alternative world view—become further marginalized.

Throughout history creative people have used their work to give form to the ineffable, to speak of ideas and emotions otherwise difficult to articulate. In this spirit, cultural producers can continue to make the invisible visible by conceiving ways to expose hidden mechanisms of censorship, and to see beneath the veil of corporate image production or government propaganda. This is a mission of engaged citizenship, a job of questioning the social arrangements we find ourselves a part of. As we encourage one another in such patterns of critical living, we begin to cultivate collective participation in public life and foster a genuine democracy in which all groups truly are free to speak.

The Published Word

As debates rage over censorship and regulated speech, a far greater threat to free expression often gets ignored. The sustenance of authoritarianism and antidemocratic politics lies in the consolidated economic strength supporting it. This is no more evident than in the concentration of media ownership in the hands of a few corporations. This effect of media consolidation was documented by

Ben J. Bagdikian in his often-quoted study of the early 1980s, *The Media Monopoly.*[11] The book opens with the following ominous prediction: "No single corporation controls all the mass media in the United States. But the daily newspapers, magazines, broadcasting systems, books, motion pictures, and most other mass media are rapidly moving in the direction of tight control by a handful of huge multinational corporations. If mergers, acquisitions, and takeovers continue at the present rate, one massive firm will be in virtual control of all major media by the 1990s."[12]

Bagdikian's vision proved prophetic in describing an ever-shrinking landscape of media ownership, where less than a handful of corporations control seventy-five percent of the leading movie studios (including Buena Vista Films, Paramount Communications, Twentieth-Century Fox, and Time Warner), seventy percent of the major radio networks (such as ABC, Capital Cities, CBS, Westinghouse, and Metromedia), and virtually all television production (like Capital Cities/ABC, CBS/QVC, NBC, and Fox). Due to mergers and acquisitions, the number of corporations continued to fall over the next two decades. Although the United States is now wired by more than eleven thousand cable television systems, the majority of the nation's millions of cable subscribers are served by seven companies (Viacom, Time Warner, and MCA, to name a few), many of which hold monopolies in the localities where they operate.[13] Not surprisingly, these very same public media are currently hyping the threat purportedly posed by the Hollywood Left. Yet as Elayne Rapping commented in *The Progressive,* this is another false alarm sounded by conservatives: "The myth that these people have, in fact, any power at all over the content of Hollywood films is ludicrous and serves to obfuscate, for an already confused public, the actual economic and political workings of the movie industry.... Racism, sexism, and the glorification of violence in the service of illegitimate power are thriving in Hollywood as never before. And the Hollywood Left has absolutely no inclination or power to do anything about it."[14]

The consequences of this media consolidation constitute more than a simple corporate juggernaut. As more and more of the communications' landscape has been gobbled up by fewer and fewer stakeholders, the effects on the nation's democracy have been a disaster. As Bagdikian explained,

> This is more than an industrial statistic. It goes to the heart of American democracy. As the world becomes more volatile, as changes accelerate and create new problems that demand new solutions, there is an urgent need for broader and more diverse sources of public information. But the reverse is happening.
>
> Today there is hardly an American industry that does not own a major media outlet, or a major media outlet grown so large that it does not own a firm in a major industry. These media report the news of industries in which they either are owners or share directors and policies.[15]

By the time the 1992 edition of *The Media Monopoly* appeared, continued mergers and buyouts had created an arena of less than two dozen companies owning ninety percent of the nation's newspapers, magazines, radio and television stations, movie and music companies, wire services, video stores, and photo agencies.[16] The Telecommunications Act of 1996 permitted even greater economies of scale, incorporating cable, satellite, computer, and Internet integration. As a result of George W. Bush's ascendancy to the White House in 2000 and the Republican Party's control of the House and Senate, this deregulatory trend continued unimpeded—and with it media consolidation intensified even further. With the Democrat's recapture of the House and Senate in the 2006 midterm elections, Congress began a series of regional town hall–style meetings to examine public attitudes toward media consolidation.

But these did not result in any legislation or structural changes of the media industries. Today, all but a small percentage of entertainment media are owned by six entities. The corporations and the notable holdings include: AOL/Time Warner (AOL, CNN, DC Comics, Time Inc., *Sports Illustrated*, Warner Brothers Television); CBS Corporation (CBS, UPN, Paramount Parks, Showtime, Simon and Schuster); Disney/Pixar (ABC Television, Disney Pictures, Touchstone Pictures, Miramax Films, ESPN, Pixar); General Electric (GE, NBC, Universal Parks and Resorts, Universal Pictures, USA Network); News Corporation (DirecTV, Fox, HarperCollins, *New York Post*, Twentieth Century Fox); Viacom (Comedy Central, DreamWorks SKG, MTV, Nickelodeon, Paramount Pictures). The effects of this corporate consolidation of media into the hands of a small number of corporations mean more than the concentration of wealth. They narrow the spectrum of programming and opinion available from public media. As Robert W. McChesney writes, "The damage has been done. Democracy is premised on a free press, and freedom of the press is premised on the absence of public or private gatekeepers with monopolistic power."[17]

Frustration over this increasingly antidemocratic consolidation of media and publishing has led many to look for futuristic solutions. Historically, technology has sparked the imagination of liberals and conservatives alike, as evidenced in the utopian speculation over the potentials of cable television. Regrettably, cable's promise of programming variety and viewer choice was undermined when its delivery system was gobbled up by commercial interests. Rather than a genuine diversity of programming options, audiences found more of the same, duplicated on endless channels. The added venues that were developed were either adapted to the commercial potentials of the new medium (MTV, CNN, TBS) or, in the case of community access cable programming, were relegated to a small and marginalized spectrum of the dial.[18]

Like cable, the information superhighway was touted as the medium that might finally realize Marshall McLuhan's dream of a global village. During the late 1960s, McLuhan attracted a devoted following based on his vision of a global telecommunications network designed on biological (and therefore natural) principles that would undermine all hierarchical structures. At the core of McLuhan's program lay a concept of media as "information without content" that defined international turmoil as the result of failed communication rather than ideological confrontation.[19] The flaw in McLuhan's reasoning lay in its formalism—its complete willingness to overlook the profit motives or political motivations of those controlling the media.

Such less-than-utopian tendencies became apparent in the scramble to develop the Internet, as megacorporations battled each other to stake claims on whatever they could get. On the more innocuous levels, this move was manifest in the rapid proliferation of electronic mail networks, (e-mail) bulletin board systems (BBSs), or sites on the World Wide Web (WWW), all of which function like post offices for sending and receiving written (and increasingly pictorial) messages. Often touted as a "free" medium of communication, the most readily accessible ways of using the Internet—AOL and Prodigy—are metered to exact a fee for every minute of use. Telephone access via computer to libraries, public archives, and databases is similarly limited to those willing to pay for service.

Even more ominous in the 2000s have been the mergers of telephone and cable television companies to combine these services in a medium. Corporate giants Bell Atlantic, Telecommunications Inc. (TCI), Time Warner, and Viacom have joined forces in deals to offer video phone services providing not only the capacity to see the person one is calling, but also a broad range of entertainment, information, business, and, most important, shopping services into the home. At issue is the fundamental difference between the telephone (which is a two-directional medium) and the cable box (which simply permits choice from among one-directional messages). Will individuals, community groups, and nonprofit organizations ever be able to broadcast their messages over the new telephone/cable information superhighway? Such decentralized capacities could have had a genuinely positive effect on the quality of U.S. democracy. But without legislation to insure such access, these services largely have gone the way of cable television.

Obviously it will take more than the recognition of this monopolistic repression to bring about change. On a discursive level, this may involve establishing new institutions, media organizations, and initiatives on the electronic frontier. Engaged citizens can take on this struggle over meaning by recognizing that the battle inheres in our everyday language. The task, then, is more than a simple contest over media control—important as that conflict is. It involves reclamation of the daily vocabulary through which the struggle is expressed. It means redefining the iconography of freedom and oppression and keeping it alive for one another. It means forging alliances by expressing the message in a clear and accessible fashion. Progressives can build a broad-based social movement from the common estrangement of consumers and other groups from power, working to banish double-speak and censorship while dispelling the internalized oppression that people sometimes carry inside themselves. This is done through groups like the ACLU, Move On, the National Coalition Against Censorship, and People for the American Way. Such work gives people a tool far more powerful than a useful lesson for a particular book or film. It's a lesson that says they have the authority (if they so choose) to challenge even the most regressive texts, to construct new meanings from such texts, and to make their own texts from the ruins of old ones.

Notes

1. Paulo Freire, *Pedagogy of the Oppressed*, 30th anniversary edition (New York: Continuum, 2000).

2. Ibid.

3. Antonio Gramsci, *Selections from the Prison Notebooks*, ed. Quinten Hoare (New York: International Publishers, 1972), 33.

4. Lisa Tiersten, *Marianne on the Market: Envisioning Consumer Society in Fin-de-Siècle* (Berkeley: University of California Press, 2001).

5. Willis, *Common Culture*.

6. Molly Ivins, untitled address, National Public Radio, June 22, 1995.

7. Cornel West, *Race Matters* (New York: Vintage Books, 1994), 19.

8. David Trend, "NEA Watch," Artpaper (Oct. 1992).

9. Gerald Allen, quoted in "We Have to Protect the People," *The Guardian*, Dec. 9, 2004. *http://arts.guardian.co.uk/features/story/0,,1369643,00.html*. Accessed Feb. 20, 2007.

10. Ibid.

11. Ben J. Bagdikian. *The Media Monopoly* (Boston: Beacon Press, 1983).

12. Ibid., 3.

13. Ibid., xii

14. Elayne Rapping, "Who Needs the Hollywood Left?" *The Progressive* 57, no. 9 (Sept. 1993), 34.

15. Bagdikian, 4.

16. Ibid.

17. Robert W. McChesney, "The National Entertainment State," *The Nation*, July 3, 2006, 18.

18. William Hoynes, *Public Television for Sale: Media, the Market, and the Public Sphere* (Boulder and San Francisco: Westview, 1994).

19. McLuhan, *Understanding Media*, 23.

Chapter Six

Building

Globalization and Democracy

This chapter examines our roles as citizens of communities and of the world. By reaffirming the old dictum to "act locally and think globally," discussion focuses on the way our everyday actions at home, school, with friends, or at a job affect democracy on a local level and also play a role in how we can begin thinking about equality and social change in the larger world. The first essay, "Acting Locally," considers how decades ago people gathered at neighborhood parks or local clubs and night spots. In the new millennium, meetings occur in chat rooms, online communities, and virtual worlds. The next essay, "Think Globally," assumes that if people are held together by what they have in common and if groups are separated by their differences, how, then, do societies and nations interact as these commonalities and differences are negotiated through laws, institutions, and behaviors. The final essay, "Democracy," considers the importance of democratic exchange and egalitarianism in human affairs. The questions asked are the following: Can democracy and its implicit commitment to discussion and an orderly means of making decisions ultimately provide a means for achieving peace on both a local and global level?

Acting Locally

How many times have we heard that people are naturally greedy? Or that it is somehow "normal" for people to act in their own self interest? Or that conflict is a natural part of human nature and that war is an inevitable part of international affairs? Such ideas have been around for a long time. They suggest that there is something unchangeable in the negative aspects of society and that any hope for long-term change is futile. Ultimately this pessimism about human nature fosters a feeling of hopelessness and underlying despair about the future.

In part, this thinking has roots in people's assumption about humankind's "natural" proclivities and its evolution from lower species. Charles Darwin promoted this view is in his book the *Origin of the Species* along with the argument that people were naturally competitive.[1] To Darwin, the elimination of weaker and less able members of a species was part of a process of "natural selection" that improved the overall species over time. The basis for "social Darwinism" actually goes back further—at least to 1776 when Adam Smith wrote *Wealth of Nations*.[2] In that book, Smith argued that people are naturally self-interested and that effective societies make use of this trait. As one of the forbearers of modern capitalism, Smith envisioned a society comprised of multitudes of small business people all acting for their own good and raising the quality of society overall. This idea of a consumer marketplace working to the benefit of society implies that when people are pursuing profit they are doing good for society.[3]

Most people don't question these basic assumptions about human nature or the appropriateness of market capitalism. These basic facts are seen as given and universal. But as Cynthia Kaufman has pointed out, in fact there is nothing natural about human self-interest and greed.[4] At best the greed hypothesis explains how people operate in business. It doesn't apply to how they act in all other aspects life. But because we live in a society so overwhelmingly infused with images of commodities, consumption, and suggestions from the media of what we need for the good life, it becomes difficult to visualize alternatives. In contrast to Darwin and Smith, progressive theorists have argued that human nature actually is more concerned with caring about other people. Proponents of this view assert that healthy societies encourage this caring sensibility. For example, Emma Goldman wrote that people naturally work to help each other, even without the structuring assistance of a government. In stark contrast to those who argue that markets embody the very essence of freedom in allowing people to buy and sell at will, Goldman proposed that true freedom could be found only outside the realm of government or the marketplace in a condition of anarchy defined as "the philosophy of a new social order based on liberty unrestricted by man-made law."[5]

Kaufman points out that thinkers from non-Western nations have frequently proposed alternatives to societies premised on competition and self-interest. In fact, the idea of people being best understood as basically individualistic is very specific to the European tradition. The Nigerian writer Segun Gbadegsin writes that people are born into social relations that dictate how they will think and relate to others, but that these relationships do not necessarily prescribe Western views of individual interests over that of the community.[6] Writing of Nigerian society in the Yoruba tradition, Gbadesgsin states that there "need not be any tension between individual and community since it is possible for an individual to freely give up his/her own perceived interest for the survival of the community." He adds "the idea of individual rights, based on a conception of individuals as atoms, is therefore bound to be foreign to this system. For the community is founded on notions of an intrinsic and enduring relationship among its members."[7]

A major difference between Smith's individualistic views and Gbadegsin's communal ideas lies in their views of freedom. These two thinkers typify proponents of what Karl Marx termed negative *freedom from* and positive *freedom to* approaches to human liberty.[8] In Marx's view, Smith espouses a negative view of freedom from external influences like government or other people. Gbadegsin's positive view of freedom gives people the unmediated ability to engage others and pursue happiness. Market capitalism promotes a negative view of freedom by pitting individuals against each other and the marketplace itself. Critics of negative freedom ask how free people can be if they need to struggle daily to get the basic items they need to survive. In a system run by the positive *freedom to* approach, more emphasis is placed on enabling people to do and get what they want without struggle and competition. If everyone shares what they need, people are free to pursue other interests.

The negative *freedom from* and positive *freedom to* approaches to liberty described by Marx have implications about how we live together in a society and how we feel about our lives. In a society where most people constantly are looking out only for themselves, any endeavor that doesn't contribute to that effort seems like a waste of time. Work can seem like a task intended primarily for earning one's salary and contributing to the general welfare of the community—paying taxes, for example—can seem like an imposition or a penalty. But to people living in a *freedom to* society, work can be seen as having a shared benefit to everyone and contributing to the general welfare of society raises the entire community's standard of living. As Kaufman writes,

> Imagine a small-scale society in which farming, cooking, mak-
> ing objects, and taking care of children are all part of a network
> of social relationships that have inherent meaning. In our own
> society even the unpleasant work, like taking out the garbage,

doesn't seem miserable when we are doing it as a favor to a friend. When human activity takes place in the context of mutually desired social relationships, none of it necessarily feels like work. Before there was a class society, there was no such thing as work. Work, meaning an alienated and meaningless way of meeting our needs, is a modern invention.[9]

In one way or another all civic compacts are defined in relationships between individual and community. Through such arrangements personal interests are balanced with a concern for the common good. Within the United States this relationship of individual to community has evolved in a particularly schizophrenic manner, as notions of success, accumulation, and liberty are conflated with themes of patriotism, philanthropy, and social justice. Indeed, it is argued that in the twentieth century, and particularly within the last decade, there has been a precipitous erosion of communal spirit. The rise of corporate capitalism has equated wealth with virtue in a trickle-down vision of civic responsibility. The exhortation of presidential candidates, "Are you better off than you were four years ago?" smacks of self-absorption. Everywhere, one is surrounded by institutions that encourage citizens to assume roles of selfish individualism—from television programs valorizing wealth and success to religious tracts promising personal salvation.

How then do alliances form among people? One way entails activating mechanisms of personal initiative that encourage people to act politically. This is what tells people that their actions have an impact in the face of governments and corporate bureaucracies. But to accomplish this task one must first examine in more detail the structures that hold such apathy and indifference to political involvement in place. Generally speaking, perhaps the three most damaging impediments to everyday democracy are objectification, rationalization, and commodification.

Objectification can be described as the process through which people come to be seen as passive and manipulable objects, rather than active and autonomous subjects. Objectification perpetuates a fatalism that tells people they can do little to alter the course of history of their own lives. This ideology of passive spectatorship is deployed in many forms, including the mass media. Movies, television, magazines, and newspapers suggest that the production of ideas and images is something that is always done by someone else. This message is perhaps most powerfully transmitted through traditional educational practices that stress a distant, immovable body of official knowledge that can only be verified and delivered by a certified teacher. It is the regressive embodiment of the Hegelian master/servant dialectic.

Rationalization is the process often associated with modernism, structuralism, and functionalism that imposes bureaucratic regulation, surveillance, and measurement to human activity for the purpose of increasing efficiency. In this scheme, people submit to a larger structure in the presumed interest of the common good. What often gets lost in the process is any sense of accountability or any ability of the individual or group to challenge the common order. Beyond being told that they cannot make a difference, this thinking implicitly tells citizens that they should not rock the boat, cause trouble, or upset the system. It suggests that disagreement is a function of individual anomaly, maladjustment, inadequacy, lack of will, or personal defect.

Commodification foregrounds valuation and exchange in life. It encourages acquisition and consumption as means of personal satisfaction, while on a larger social scale promoting hierarchies among people. On a broader scale, commodification frustrates community ethos by encouraging competitive acquisition. Debilitating fictions of "making it" and "the good life" are defined in terms of solitary consumption rather than civic concern. The first strategy in combating such thinking is to raise the question of how well off the average citizen is, posing this question to those who have suffered the consequences of economic violence. Given the glaring lack of equality in the United States, one can't help asking why more people aren't clamoring for radical change. Maybe it has to do with the perception that the task is so overwhelming. Or perhaps it results from the lack of a meaningful program. At the very least, people concerned about commodified thinking can encourage the growing rage of all citizens silenced by the illusion of our purportedly egalitarian nation. As Kobena Mercer has pointed out, for every idealized scene of flag-waving jubilation, there is a non-idealized scene of lived oppression, discrimination, and economic violence.[10] With each passing year the distance between the dream and the reality widens. The reckoning that is coming holds both possibilities and potential difficulties for building a sense of community.

Where does the process begin? By proceeding with sensitivity and care. One of the most important cautions for people interested in social change involves the tendency to slip into moralizing dogma. For activists this means beginning with a reconsideration of the very ways one goes about articulating issues. In part, this means a reexamination of the concept of audience. Exactly who is the presumed public for social change? Does such a singularly defined constituency even exist? If not, how can any speaker address the interests of a diverse people? These issues of authority and address must be resolved to effect strategies for democratic society.

In theorizing a democracy that acknowledges the complexities of these circumstances, we must incorporate an acceptance of groups' different needs and a recognition of the contested character of healthy democracy.[11] This type of democracy admits the struggle that results from difference, but counts it as a positive force in the continual testing and reevaluation of political arrangements. As Mercer notes, "What is at issue is to acknowledge differences without necessarily ending up in a divisive situation, how to enact an 'ethics of disagreement,' as Hall says, without recourse to rhetorics that cut off the possibility of critical dialogue."[12] No single set of ideas is privileged over others because no one method can satisy the needs of a diverse people.

The battle really takes place on two fronts. First, on the level of public communication, progressives need to confront efforts to depoliticize and dehistoricize social forms. All too often status-quo interests have been permitted to label selected territories off-limits to political debate and thereby silence or discredit oppositional work. In this context, the first gesture of progressive activists is to bring to public light underexamined regions of oppression. Second, at the more crucial level of oppositional practices, the job entails seizing means (or inventing new means) to encourage diverse identities, promote the development of communities, and foster forms of respectful solidarity among them. This means doing whatever it takes to win the argument, get the job, or organize the boycott to make material change happen.

Implementing these efforts will entail a struggle. History has demonstrated that power is rarely yielded willingly. As Paulo Freire so insightfully pointed out two decades ago, it is the responsibility of the oppressed to teach their oppressors a new way of organizing society.[13] This is not always a comfortable process. A radicalized democracy admits the necessity of such struggle and the need for various communities to seek their own objectives. These are exactly the programs that some conservative groups have tried to discredit in the name of a purportedly colorless society. Such views are predicated on outmoded views of community as monolithic and static. The conservative position fails to recognize the partial, overlapping, and indeterminate character of certain communities in relation to intersections of race, age, sexual orientation, class position, nationality, occupation, geography, and so on.

In contrast, it is important to realize that members of a community can belong to many different subgroups simultaneously and to various degrees. It is equally important to avoid generalizing about communities that have dramatic internal subdivisions. There are no single definitions of feminists, rappers, religious fundamentalists, business executives, or hospital patients—only singular *representations* of these groups. These narrow representations can produce stereotypes, as mainstream discourses both mediate and discredit diversity. For this reason the politics of representation constitutes a profound ground of struggle.

Thinking Globally

Obvious as it is to recognize ways that we inhabit local communities, we are also all citizens of the world. But because of the enormity of the concept, it has become commonplace to think and act as though we are not part of the larger world. It is difficult to imagine how one's daily actions might have consequences for the global environment or how the automobiles we drive contribute to ozone depletion, global warming, and climate change. One hears about the growing intensity of hurricanes or the incremental shrinkage of glaciers, but these occurrences seem intangible and abstract. Moreover, many Americans believe that the fears about global pollution and environmental devastation are unreasonable or overblown. Two decades ago, eighty percent of people surveyed agreed that "protecting the environment is so important that standards cannot be too high and continuing environmental improvements must be made regardless of cost."[14] By the 1990s, attitudes had changed, with half of those surveyed believing that environmentalists "had gone too far." Many people believe that the world simply is too big for human culture to change in any significant way. In part, this is because the consequences of local actions on the larger world are rarely experienced directly.

Much of what takes place in distant lands seems to have little impact on our day-to-day lives. In economic terms, it is difficult to take seriously mounting national trade deficits when their immediate impact on the things we do every day is hard to discern. The implications of trade imbalances are obscured even further by the ongoing practice of the United States—especially during the Bush presidency—to forestall their consequences by allowing the nation to finance the deficits by continual borrowing from trade partners like China and Mexico. Rather than worrying people with rising prices at the grocery store, this practice of national borrowing, in effect since the 1970s, allows U.S. citizens to pay lower prices for the goods they consume than people earning equivalent wages in foreign nations. Currently the 8.6 trillion dollar federal debt of the United States is approximately $30,000 per citizen.[15] The major recent contributor to this debt has been the U.S. war in Iraq, estimated to have added 2 trillion dollars to the monetary imbalance when all of its related costs are tabulated.[16]

In a similar fashion, because military conflicts with other nations are typically waged far from U.S. soil, Americans increasingly feel insulated from global politics and military violence. Despite a slight decrease immediately following September 2001, U.S. public opinion favoring an isolationist approach to the rest of the world continues to rise. According to a 2005 Gallup poll, forty-two percent of respondents agree with the view that the "United States should mind its own business internationally and let other countries get along the best they can on their own."[17] According to the Pew poll, this represents an all-time high. That constitutes a sharp shift, and according to the Pew numbers, most of it took place in the last several years as Americans have become thoroughly disillusioned with the Iraq war. As might be expected, the public is also increasingly hostile to international institutions. Since 2002, the percentage of Americans believing that the United States "should cooperate fully with the United Nations" has fallen from sixty-seven to fifty-four percent, and the proportion wanting the United States to go its "own way in international matters … whether countries agree or not" has risen from twenty-five to thirty-two percent.[18]

Such isolationist views have a long history in the United States. Their genesis can be traced to early settlements of North America in the 1600s, when people often traveled or immigrated to the New World to escape persecution in Europe, to establish colonial lands, or to build a way of life different from what they had known. George Washington in his "Farewell Address" placed the accent on isolationism in a manner that would be long remembered: "The great rule of conduct for us, in regard to foreign nations, is in extending our commercial relations, to have with them as little political connection as possible," Washington said, adding, "Europe has a set of primary interests, which to us have none, or a very remote relation."[19]

The geographic separation of the American continents truly did permit a life of international isolation in the days before airplanes and electronic communication. This separation provided a rationale for public opposition to nearly every international involvement in the history of the United States. During the 1800s, the United

States began reaching beyond its North American territory to piece together an empire in the Caribbean and the Pacific without departing from the traditional perspective. It fought the War of 1812, the Mexican War, and the Spanish-American War without joining alliances or fighting in Europe. This legacy engendered a belief in the "natural" separation of the United States from the world and its problems that continues to influence thinking today. Indeed, in the 2000 U.S. presidential race, then-candidate Bush expressed his unequivocal opposition to the kind of U.S. involvement with other countries he termed "nation-building." In his campaign debate with Al Gore, Bush was asked if he thought intervention in establishment of foreign states was appropriate for the United States. Bush replied, "I don't think so. I think what we need to do is convince people who live in the lands they live in to build the nations. Maybe I'm missing something here. I mean, we're going to have kind of a nation-building core from America? Absolutely not. Our military is meant to fight and win war. That's what it's meant to do. And when it gets overextended, morale drops."[20]

Obviously, history has told a different story. The interconnectedness of international economies and effects of conflicts on global stability have demanded the involvement of the United States. This global perspective emerged with great multilateral support following the First and Second World Wars, with the founding of the League of Nations and the United Nations to function as international forums for the discussion of global problems and the enforcement of international accords. Following World War II, the threat embodied by the Soviet Union under Joseph Stalin dampened any comeback of isolationism. In the postwar environment, the United States played a leading role in promoting international trade, cultural exchange, expanded information systems, advanced military cooperation, and its own international dominance. A few leaders would rise to speak of a return to America's traditional policies of nonintervention, but in reality traditional U.S. isolationism was obsolete.

Can isolationism ever stage a comeback? After all, the United States is itself a nation comprised of peoples from nations all around the globe. From the precolonial days of intercontinental land migration and the explorations of the Vikings to the great European migrations of the 1600s and 1800s to the even greater international migrations to the United States of the twentieth century, "Coming to America" was the defining ethos. Immigration boomed to a 57.4 percent increase in foreign-born population from 1990 to 2000.[21] But not everyone thought highly of this growth. In the 1990s, concern began to grow in some circles about existing immigration law and immigration outside the law, especially the approximately 7.5 million illegal so-called alien workers with twelve million household members already inside the United States and another seven hundred thousand predicted for each coming year. At issue was whether the immigration laws and enforcement system were working as the public wanted them to work. Undocumented workers from Mexico alone were estimated at more than 8 million.[22] Fears about possible security threats posed by immigrants grew after September 2001, allowing immigration reform to become a hot-button issue among headline-hungry politicians. Proposals were put forward in the House of Representatives to criminalize illegal immigrants and to build an immigrant barrier along some or all of the two-thousand-mile border between the United States and Mexico. In 2006, Congress voted to approve the U.S.–Mexico "fence" without allocating funds for its construction. Despite its significance as a real or symbolic deterrent to the flow of immigrants into the United States, the concept of the fence does nothing to address the reasons why people cross the border. Wage inequities between the two countries, the availability of jobs in the United States, and the need of employers in

American border states for workers remain unaddressed in most quick-fix political solutions.

Continued immigration is one of the major ways the United States remains truly a part of the global community. The rise of multinational corporations is another. In the new global economy it has become increasingly difficult to speak about "national" industries, and large companies continue to merge and restructure their operations and manufacturing across national borders. International trade has made nations dependent upon each other for the materials to manufacture goods, the labor pools to assemble them, and the markets to buy and sell the products. Underlying much of the tension over conflicts in the Middle East is the unabated dependence of industrialized nations on imported oil. For this reason alone, the basic facts of globalization and role of nations in the global community are unlikely to change any time soon. But arguments wage over the new and relatively recent restructuring of the world into a global economy and whether international culture is good or bad.

The Pros and Cons of Globalization

What could be better than a world of seamless markets, instantaneous communication, and a global culture that is increasingly homogeneous? Many proponents of globalization say that nothing could be better. One of the most widely read proponents of globalization is *New York Times* reporter and columnist Thomas L. Friedman, who in his books *The Lexus and the Olive Tree* (2000) and the *World is Flat* (2006) asserted that the positive manifestations of globalization have been in three domains: economics, technology, and culture. Friedman explains that in economic terms, the driving idea behind globalization is free-market capitalism. To

Friedman, the more that markets open international economies to free trade and competition, the more efficient and robust those economies become. Globalization has resulted in the expansion of free trade and capitalism across the world, deregulating and privatizing national economies as it has grown. The result has been a transformation of the world from a jumble of isolated local economies into an integrated and connected single globalized marketplace. This has resulted in greater efficiencies and a huge overall expansion of the world economics system. According to Friedman, one hundred years ago capital expenditures among nations could be measured in the hundreds of millions of dollars and relatively few countries were involved. Today, private capital from the developed world into all emerging markets exceeds $205 billion. "This new era of globalization, compared to the one before World War I, is turbocharged."[23]

Turning to technologies, the new globalization is defined by computerization, miniaturization, digitization, satellite communications, fiber optics, and the Internet. Such forms of technology present a fundamentally new and unique ethos of globalization. In contrast to a Cold War world typified by separation and division, the defining paradigms of globalization are unity and integration. The symbols of the Cold War were geographical distances and national boundaries, which divided people from each other. The symbol of the new globalization is the World Wide Web, which connects everyone. Today's globalization has been enabled by the falling costs of electronic communications for things like microchips, satellites, and fiber optics. New and inexpensive modes of communication have brought the nations of the world together as never before. These technologies also allow companies to locate different parts of their production, research, and marketing in different countries but still tie them together through computers and teleconferencing, as though they were in one place. Moreover, due to the combination of computers and cheap communications, nations everywhere can enter and compete in the global marketplace of electronic commerce, media production, and the information economy. Globalization also is a huge cultural phenomenon. Friedman argues that this has meant that isolated or formerly backward nations are no longer cut off from the ideas and philosophies of developed countries. In part, this is an outgrowth of enhanced communications in areas like telecommunications, cable and satellite television, and electronic publishing of CDs and DVDs. But it also results from the increased movement of people from rural areas to urban areas. At no time in history has it been so easy for people to travel or migrate from one place to another.

Not everyone is happy with globalization. Opponents of globalization say it leads to exploitation of the world's poor and the devastation of the environment. A report by the Alternatives Committee of the International Forum on Globalization asserts that the "unrestricted movement of capital" generates enormous profits for transnational corporations but produces significant economic, social, and political harms for the majority of nations and peoples.[24] This report finds that global well-being is threatened—not fostered—by the conversion of national economies to export-oriented production, the increasing concentration of corporate wealth, and the decreasing regulation of corporate behavior. Moreover, globalization is seen as undermining social and environmental programs within nations, as well as contributing to the "privatization and commodification" of public services, the erosion of "traditional powers and policies of democratic nation-states and local communities," and the "unrestricted exploitation of the planet's resources."[25] Needless to say, opponents to globalization argue that while it may enable corporations like Wal-Mart to make $29 DVD players available to customers in the United States, it does so only through manufacturing practices that underpay workers in poor nations.

While some inexpensive DVD players in the United States might be seen as increasing the distribution of new technology, enormous disparities still exist in technological access worldwide. This gap in capacity has been termed the "digital divide." In 2005, the United Nations reported that despite the fact that there are many Internet cafés and other access points in low-income countries, a person in a high-income country is twenty-two times more likely to be an Internet user than one in a low-income country.[26] This is significant because thirty-seven percent of the world population lives in low-income countries. Moreover, the cost of slow, unreliable Internet service in a low-income country is greater than the cost of fast, reliable service in a high-income country. In fact, Internet affordability is more than 150 times greater in a high-income than a low-income country.[27]

But economics and technology are only part of the problem. For many critics of globalization, the most serious threats posed are environmental. According to Arthur Lyon Dahl of the United Nations Environment Program (UNEP), as the world's population has grown and the leverage provided by technology has increased, our impacts on the environment have reached the global scale. On one level, humanity has negatively affected the world by polluting it. We have released enough carbon dioxide and other greenhouse gases to have a measurable effect on global climate, while chlorofluorocarbons (CFCs) and other synthetic gases have attacked and depleted the ozone layer. Globally distributed pesticides have an impact on hormonal balances and the immune systems in both people and animals. On another level, the problem has been exacerbated by the consumption of natural resources. The globalization of trade puts pressure on natural resources around the world, helping to drive the rapid depletion of tropical forests, the collapse of many ocean fisheries, and even the global impoverishment of biological diversity. Finally, the diffusion of human culture has contributed to the spread of epidemics and the growing problem of antibiotic resistance. As Dahl explains, "Little attention has been paid to the synergies and interactions between environmental problems, and between them and social and economic systems that may, in fact, represent some of the biggest future problems and surprises."[28] Dahl adds, "While it has always been possible to escape from environmental limits at a local or national scale, the planet is a closed system (except for solar energy) and there is no escape from planetary limits."[29]

There also is no escape from the cultural consequences of globalization through the processes of what is termed "cultural transfer." On a basic level, culture moves from one land to another in the processes of human migration, trade, and through the dissemination of media. But this is never a neutral process because pressures exist between and within nations that favor certain cultures over others. Generally this means that newcomers need to adopt and assimilate to whatever culture they enter. But it can also signal a change or assault on a home culture when the outsiders resist change. For example, the colonial and industrialized nations have often been accused of "cultural imperialism," based on the assumption that powerful countries will force their culture, ideology, goods, and way of life on another country. Critics accusing the United States of cultural imperialism have claimed that the nation makes a conscious effort to export American culture abroad in order to gain access to raw materials, cheap labor, and new markets for U.S. consumer products.

9/11

September 11 provided the ultimate negative example of globalization in action. The stories and famous footage of the World Trade Center towers collapsing occupied all of the major networks for four straight days, during which all other programming was suspended. Much is made of the uniqueness of the moment—of the way September 11 forever changed the way the United States viewed itself. Introducing *The Age of Terror*, one of dozens of books to appear on the topic of September 11, John Lewis Gaddis solemnly states, "Whatever we eventually settle on calling the events of September 11—the Attack on America, Black Tuesday, 9/11—they've already forced a reconsideration, not only of where we are as a nation and where we might be going, but also of where we've been, even who we are."[30]

While emotionally satisfying to dwell on the exceptional scale of the assaults, much of the discourse seemed oddly familiar. This is because the entertainment industry had already depicted fictional events so similar to the September 11 attack that many viewers remarked how like a movie the footage seemed. Adopting familiar motifs, journalists wrote a violent narrative of good versus evil and us versus them—complete with a nefarious evildoer of a leader. Ironically, as the dust has settled over 9/11 and the years have begun to pass, the entertainment industry has ghoulishly revisited the tragedy with films like *The Path to 9/11* (2005), *United 93* (2006), *World Trade Center* (2006), and *Live Free or Die Hard* (2007).

The novelty of the assaults created an atmosphere devoid of any criticality whatsoever, due in large part to the networks' fear that the appearance of an unpatriotic opinion would mean lost advertising revenue. This has produced an atmosphere in which alternative perspectives were rarely reported and, as a consequence, rarely debated in public. This meant that those seeking a range of opinion had to look elsewhere. The good news has been that the topic of terrorism became a huge Internet phenomenon, with hundreds of sites providing divergent perspectives. In a similar fashion, the post-9/11 tunnel vision of mainstream news has enlivened independent publishing and media production. People are looking to alternative media and the Internet insight with an urgency that was missing prior to the attacks.

Ultimately this broadening of the discourse is the answer to the global media violence dilemma. The problem isn't that we have too much violence in movies and TV. The problem is that the kind of violence portrayed is so limited. Due to the consolidation of production into the hands of a few giant multinational corporations, decision making is conducted by a small number of executives who are mostly white, mostly male, and who are driven by the need to make a profit. This economic imperative to reach huge audiences through extremely polished and expensive programs eliminates the willingness to take risks or to deviate from proven formulas. So the world gets violent media of a very particular kind—aesthetized to maximize its accessibility and its capacity to stimulate viewers—and endlessly repeated stories of male strength and good old-fashioned American power. And it really isn't hurting anyone that much, at least not directly. Instead it's doing something much more pernicious. The mass production of media violence is wasting an enormous resource that might otherwise be capable of tremendous public good. Around the globe people learn about the world and form their understandings of it to a great extent from public culture. They gather from it the material they need to function as citizens and to participate in the civic processes. The reduction of media discourse to a redundant series of violent spectacles does something much worse than teaching people and nations to become aggressive. It tells them to do nothing.

Democracy

Democracy is a relative term. Like any other expression, its meaning in everyday life is a matter of interpretation, debate, and contest—and in recent years it is a word we have heard a great deal: from the "democratic" protests in Tiannamen Square, to the democratic reforms throughout Eastern Europe, to efforts to bring democracy to Iraq. While rival ideologies seem ever more flawed and uncertain, evidence abounds of the so-called triumph of liberal democracy. As a term nearly synonymous with the foreign policy objectives of the United States government, democracy has witnessed the fall of many who once vowed to stand in its way. Perhaps not so coincidentally, it is also nearly always equated with the global economic order of market capitalism.

These apparent contradictions in U.S. democracy suggest more than a simple gap between theory and practice. They signify the profoundly fictional character that the democratic ideal has assumed in the public mind. The very slipperiness of the term has permitted its exploitation by a range of politicians, bureaucrats, and philosophers for purposes ranging from electoral sloganeering to military intervention. For this reason an initial step in the salvaging of participatory politics may well entail an analysis of democracy's crisis of meaning. This involves asking such questions as whether democracy functions primarily as a form of decision making or as an instrument of popular empowerment, whether democracy constitutes an abstract ideal or an achievable goal, or whether democracy emerges from within a group or can be externally imposed.

Such questions begin to suggest that the very idea of a single democracy is a fallacy. Instead, democracy serves as a marker for a wide variety of interests, philosophies, and political programs expressed in the continual flux of labels like direct democracy, liberal democracy, juridical democracy, associative democracy, socialist democracy, and radical democracy, among numerous others. At the same time, these questions throw into relief the way democracy has become essentialized as an undefined norm—joining such ambiguous expressions as mainstream opinion and family values, which lack clear definitions, yet are highly effective in discrediting selected groups. It is therefore in the interest of democratic ideals to attempt to unpack the various discourses of democracy.

One way of envisioning democracy is at the end of a participatory continuum, the other end of which marks the complete exclusion of people from their common decision making. Yet contrary to much contemporary rhetoric, even this simple view of democracy also implies a set of limits on human behavior—a series of restraints on freedom itself. Any subscription to democracy presupposes a degree of faith in the possibility of politics—a belief that human need can be addressed within communities, as opposed to the anarchy of absolute privacy, liberty, and individualism. Put this way, debates over different forms of democracy all boil down to arguments over what kind of common compacts are desirable or possible in a given society.

Like other social formations, democracy is enabled by the agents of the populous who call it into being. Classical theory located this agency in the category of the citizen, bound in a contractual relationship with the state to cede certain freedoms for corresponding rights. The exact terms of this contract vary with the form of democracy used. With direct or "pure" democracies, citizens engage in common decision making without the mediation of a legislature or other representative body. Such democratic structures originated on nearly every continent, although the first written records of such practices are commonly attributed to the ancient Greeks. This privileging of Athenian democracy over other "preliterate" models has become a matter of no small consequence in its historic deployment to assert the primacy of Western civilization and to justify its natural posture of dominance.

Related to these questions about representation are similar debates about the fairness of majority rule. Classical participatory theory holds that, although decisions are made in winner-take-all voting, the regularity of polling assures that no majority is permanent. If any agreement proves inadequate it will be overturned in a subsequent ballot. For this reason, any majority has reason to remain sensitive to the needs of the minority. In practice, however, majorities have often used their political leverage to maintain their dominance. Commentators from Alexis de Tocqueville to Lani Guinier have criticized this fundamental precept of democracy for its inability to fairly represent all citizens.[31] The frequently evoked concept of the "tyranny of the majority" results, not only from winner-take-all electoral systems, but from the persistent failure of democracies to enfranchise potential voters without discrimination.

Critiques of this essentialized view of democracy often begin by pointing to the internal contradictions of Athenian society. Although credited with the invention of democracy, ancient Greece permitted only one social group access to this sanctified realm. All citizens may have had equal and unmediated participation in civic life, but women, slaves, and non-Greeks were excluded from the fraternity of citizenship. Far from a mere historical "problem" in classical democracy, this very issue of who counts as a voting citizen has plagued Western democracies ever since. It is important to point out that even within the United States—the purported model of world democracy—such a fundamental issue as women's suffrage was contested well into the twentieth century. Even these advances remained in question in such enlightened nations as Germany, Italy, and Spain, where the right to vote was systematically withheld from certain groups for subsequent decades. The denial of voting rights within the United States to African Americans and other immigrant groups remained a point of severe acrimony through the 1950s and 1960s. Problems with other immigrant groups persist today.

Despite these problems, Athenian direct democracy retains relevance for many as a philosophical ideal. The notion of active citizenship as a defining principle of public life informs many contemporary debates over issues ranging from radical pluralism to communitarianism. Indeed, contemporary exhortations about public service in the name of the national family emanate from a nostalgic yearning for a preliberal sense of civic responsibility. At issue is the degree to which direct democracy or active citizenship can be realized in massive post-industrial societies. Such idealized political models flourished in the relatively immobile atmospheres of small, oral societies in which face-to-face meetings constituted an organic part of daily life. But as European society became more complex, so did its forms of democracy. With the decline of the Roman Empire, the era of classical Italian republicanism marked a transition to elected leadership and along with it the beginning of a gradual distancing of civic governance from the citizenry. Rome's mixed government, with its interlocking system of consuls and people's tribunals, became a model for an intermediate form of democracy, in which the people remained the ultimate source of accountability, but in which forms of representation became a necessity.

The ethical dimensions of this transition from direct democracy cannot be overstated, for the shift to representative forms of government signaled a weakening of the sense of individual responsibility in community governance. The profound influence of the Christian church in the Middle Ages displaced secular morality as a motivation for involved citizenship. The prospect of divine reward helped undermine any sense of urgency about earthly problems. At the same time, religion helped foster forms of community identification that would ultimately become a separate territory of civic life. As a result, the increasingly atomized quality of secular society called for new forms of political organization that could accommodate and contain individualism and competition.

Liberal democracy evolved in direct response to the perceived encroachment of the state on personal liberty. At the center of the liberal democratic ethos lies the Western notion of the autonomous individual capable of free choice and motivated by capitalistic self-interest. Most important is the separability of existence into public and private domains. The public comprises the arena of laws, legislatures, and other civic structures, whose ultimate logic is reducible to an apolitical ideal of the common good.[32] The formation of a disinterested and distinct public sphere reveals the uniquely Western belief in Cartesian epistemology—a belief in the possibility of a knowable independent ground apart from humanity's base instincts. The transcendental universalism of the public sphere is the antithesis of the self-interested specificity of the private realm of personal interests and market competition.

The unifying element for many liberal democratic theorists is the belief that individual interest can be enhanced by mutual cooperation. As John Locke put it, "The great and chief end therefore of men uniting into commonwealths and putting themselves under government ... is the mutual preservation of their lives, liberties, and estates, which shall call by the general name property."[33] This impulse for accumulation is both enabled and limited by the state. Hence, liberal democracy assumes a two-stroke function as a justification and limit for the exercise of state authority. Regular elections serve the philosophical goal of obliging the public to clarify public issues while assuring that no government or set of public officials would remain in office forever.

Opinions differ among liberal democrats over how much the general consensus should apply to all citizens. This is both the rationale for local government and the reasoning behind various pluralist versions of liberal democracy. Pluralists agree that different groups deserve different degrees of influence over various matters according to the proportion of their interest in them. Within the liberal logic of self-interest, people are more likely to exercise their agency as citizens over matters that affect them most directly.

This principle has led some liberals to advocate a strengthening of the civil society as a means of decentralizing democracy and lessening the role of the state. The civil society argument, occasionally termed the "associationalist" view, asserts that the goals of social justice and human welfare are best served by voluntary and self-governing private bodies, such as unions, political parties, religious organizations, schools, neighborhood groups, clubs, and societies.[34] This position gained popularity in the Western world during the nineteenth century but was squeezed out of existence with the growing dominance of collectivist and individualist politics. Although similar to liberal democracy, this view differs in according voluntary bodies a primary role in organizing social life, rather that an ancillary function to government. These smaller, private entities, which may or may not be governed by democratic principles, are viewed as more flexible and responsive to community needs. Representative government assumes a regulatory function as guarantor of services, rather than acting as their provider. Limited to this oversight role, government bureaucracy is lessened and its efficiency enhanced as a consequence.

A related trend has been the growing popularity of communitarianism, in which the ethical dimensions of voluntarism are emphasized over the mandates of self-interest. As espoused by Amitai Etzioni and William Gallston, the trouble with conventional liberalism is that it focuses too much on individual rights and not enough on shared values.[35] To overcome these problems, communitarians suggest that people should become more involved in developing the social glue that holds society together through such entities as schools, neighborhoods, and the family. If democracy is conceptualized as a series of compromises between individual and collective interest, socialist democracy clearly leans in the latter direction. Critical of the liberal emphasis on competition, Karl Marx and Fredrich Engles viewed material inequities, not merely as by-products of such a model, but also necessary components of it. To create winners in the game of acquisition, a system must also generate losers. The much-ballyhooed opportunities for liberty offered by liberal capitalism mean little if they are not universally accessible. The inequities produced by capital in turn spoil the very functioning of democracy, as the state becomes little more than the tool of the privileged. In this scheme, the very idea of a separation between private and public is thrown into question. Rather than serving as an idealized and apolitical mediator of the common good, government is perverted by the ability of some citizens to exert more control over it than others.

Democracy for Everyday People

Although history has shown that democracy can be frustrated and at times derailed, the cause cannot be abandoned. One place to continue the work lies in the everyday. The principles of what has been termed "radical democracy" assert that democracy can be restored on all levels of society by beginning with democracy in the smallest moments of daily existence. The democratic project needn't begin with a grandiose national strategy, but can instead emerge on the shop floor, in the classroom, or at the dinner table where tactics begin to play out. Theorists Ernesto Laclau and Chantal Mouffe proposed what they called a radical democratic concept of the citizen defined by the multiple subjectivities and atomized encounters of daily life. Far from a unified autonomous social actor, within this formulation each person find oneself in a continual flow of democratic moments and opportunities. According to Laclau and Mouffe, constantly changing social dynamics provide continual openings for the creation of new political spaces.[36] In this expanded view of democracy, the very definition of the political becomes broadened to a new range of sites across the domain of cultural representations and social practices.

In such a context, this poststructuralist approach to pluralism does not negate popular engagement with democracy as it is often accused of doing. Instead, by opening new territory, the model gives new vitality to the impetus for democratic principles. The politicization of social spaces formerly considered neutral makes apparent the often unacknowledged power relations in everyday activities. In this way, such off-limits territories as culture, education, and the family become sites of critical investigation and emancipatory possibility. Rather than diminishing a sense of political agency, the principles of radical democracy have the potential of reinvigorating the subject within new domains of influence. Just as importantly, in arguing against the notion of a fixed or universal subject, the project of a radical democracy is by definition never complete.[37] But while the task may seem daunting in the endless horizon it establishes, incremental progress can be measured in everyday victories. It is through these daily advances that we make progress and keep hope alive.

The principles of radical democracy provide a reminder of the potentials inherent in everyday activities. While acknowledging the importance of large political institutions, radical democracy urges people to recognize the "personal is political." Not only do individuals interact with political processes in collective acts like voting and work with political parties, they also practice forms of politics at home, in school, at the workplace, and among groups of friends. In this way, democracy becomes more than something discussed on the nightly news. It inheres in the way people live their lives, structure their relationships, and organize into groups. It's meaning becomes known and experienced through its everyday forms and applications. As discussed throughout this book, the everyday becomes a medium through which people come to know politics, economics, and other forces that act upon people and their societies. It is through the everyday that people most persuasively come to find and make meaning in the world.

Considerations of democracy bring *Everyday Culture* full-circle—back to ordinary life. Debating democracy across the dinner table in many ways is as important as democracy practiced in the voting booth. *Everyday Culture* has aspired to draw attention to the often-perceived gap between what takes place in personal experiences and the larger forces and institutions that can seem beyond human scale. In this sense, the discussion has taken the ordinary and intentionally politicized it, or, more accurately, called attention to its inherent politics. The common dismissal of ordinary culture as insignificant permits the removal of everyday relations of inequality or acts of bias from serious scrutiny. The personal and seemingly inconsequential politics that take place in the home, at school, or in the workplace indeed do matter because they undergird and enable the larger politics of life. Apathy, alienation, and perceptions of powerlessness begin in the micropolitics of everyday experience. So do inclinations of concern, engagement, and social activism. Everyday culture is where these begin and end.

Notes

1. Charles Darwin, *Origin of the Species* (New York: Prometheus Books, 1975).

2. Adam Smith, *Wealth of Nations* (New York: Modern Library, 1994).

3. Cynthia Kaufman, *Ideas for Action: Relevant Theory for Radical Change* (Boston: South End Press, 2003), 9.

4. Ibid., 10.

5. Ibid., 13.

6. Segun Gbadegsin, as cited in *Ideas for Action,* 15.

7. Ibid.

8. Karl Marx, *The Philosophic and Economic Manuscripts of 1844* (New York: Prometheus Books, 1988).

9. Kaufman, 18.

10. Kobena Mercer, "Welcome to the Jungle: Identity and Diversity in Postmodern Politics," in Jonathan Rutherford, ed., *Identity: Community, Culture, Difference* (London Lawrence and Wishart, 1990), 43–71.

11. Chantal Mouffe, "Radical Democracy: Modern or Postmodern?" in *Universal Abandon? The Politics of Postmodernism,* ed. Andrew Ross (Minneapolis: University of Minnesota Press, 1988), 42.

12. Lorraine Kenny, "Traveling Theory: An Interview with Kobena Mercer," in *Afterimage* 18, no. 2 (Sept. 1990): 9.

13. Freire.

14. David Edwards, book review of *Global Spin: The Corporate Assault on Environmentalism,* by Sharon Beder, *Z Magazine,* July 1998, *http://www.zmag.org/zmag/articles/global_spinjuly98.htm.* Accessed Dec. 12, 2006.

15. U.S. National Debt Clock. *http://www.brillig.com/debt_clock/.* Accessed Dec. 12, 2007.

16. David Welna, "Congress Sets New Federal Debt Limit: $9 Trillion," *http://www.NPR.org.* Accessed Dec. 12, 2006.

17. John B. Judis, cited in "Isolationism on the Rise," Atlantic Review Online, Dec. 27, 2005. *http://atlanticreview.org/archives/222-Isolationism-on-the-rise.html.* Accessed. Dec 12, 2006.

18. Ibid.

19. "World Affairs: Isolationism," at U.S. History.com. *http://www.u-s-history.com/pages/h1601.html.* Accessed Dec 13, 2006.

20. "Candidate Bush on Nation Building," on *Pierre Le Grands' Pink Flamingo Bar,* http://pierrelegrand.net/2006/10/18/islam-cartoons-secularism-and-individual-freedom-can-islam-and-democracy-survive-one-another.htm. Accessed Dev. 14, 2006.

21. "Immigration to the United States," Wikipedia. *http://*

en.wikipedia.org/wiki/Immigration_to_the_United_States. Accessed Dec. 14, 2006.

22. Ibid.

23. Thomas L. Friedman, excerpt from *The Lexus and the Olive Tree*. *http://www.thomaslfriedman.com/lexusolivetree.htm*. Accessed Dec. 16, 2006

24. As cited in David Michael Smith, "The Growing Revolt Against Globalization." *http://www.impactpress.com/articles/augsep02/globaliza-tion8902.html*. Accessed Dec. 18, 2006.

25. Ibid.

26. U.N. Conference on Trade and Development, *The Digital Divide Report: ICT Diffusion Index 2005. http://www.unctad.org/en/docs/iteipc20065_en.pdf.* Accessed Dec. 18, 2006

27. Ibid.

28. Arthur Lyon Dahl, "Globalization and the Environment," in Proceedings of the conference Globalization: A Challenge for Peace or Exclusion? October 1998. *http://www.bcca.org/ief/ddahl98b.htm*. Accessed Dec. 18, 2006.

29. Ibid.

30. John Lewis Gaddis, "And Now This: Lessons from the Old Era for the New One," in *The Age of Terror: America and the World After September 11,* eds. Strobe Talbott and Nayan Chandra (New York: Basic Books, 2002), 11.

31. Alexis de Tocqueville, *Democracy in America* (New York: A.A. Knopf, 1945); Lani Guinier, *The Tyranny of the Majority: Fundamental Fairness in Representative Democracy* (New York: Free Press, 1994).

32. John Dewey, *Democracy and Education: An Introduction to the Philosophy of Education* (New York: Macmillan, 1944); John Rawls, *A Theory of Justice* (Cambridge: Harvard University Press, 1971).

33. John Locke, *The Second Treatise of Civil Government* (Buffalo: Prometheus Books, 1986), 413.

34. Michael Walzer, "The Civil Society Argument," in *Dimensions of Radical Democracy,* ed. Chantal Mouffe (London and New York; Verso, 1991), 89–107; Paul Hirst, "Associational Democracy," in *Prospects for*

Democracy: North/South/East/West, ed. David Held (Stanford: Stanford University Press, 1993), 112–135.

35. Amitai Etzioni, *Capital Corruption: The New Attack on American Democracy* (New Brunswick: Transaction Books, 1988); Amitai Etzioni, *The Spirit of Community: Rights, Responsibilities, and The Communitarian Agenda* (New York: Crown Books, 1993).

36. Laclau and Mouffe, *Hegemony and Socialist Strategy.*

37. Noam Chomsky, "Democracy's Slow Death," *In These Times* 19, no. 1 (Nov. 28–Dec. 11, 1994), 25.

INDEX

✳

ABOUT THE AUTHOR

David Trend is Professor of Studio Art at the University of California–Irvine. He is the author of *The Myth of Media Violence* (Blackwell 2007).